LIPPINCOTT'S

CABINET HISTORIES.

VIRGINIA.

PHILADELPHIA.
LIPPINCOTT, GRAMBO & Co.
1852.

Lippincott's

Cabinet Histories of the States.

VIRGINIA.

THE

HISTORY OF VIRGINIA,

FROM ITS

Earliest Settlement to the Present Time.

BY

T. S. ARTHUR

AND

W. H. CARPENTER.

PHILADELPHIA:
LIPPINCOTT, GRAMBO & CO.
1853.

STEREOTYPED BY L. JOHNSON AND CO.
PHILADELPHIA.
PRINTED BY T. K. AND P. G. COLLINS.

PUBLISHERS' PREFACE.

There are but few persons in this country who have not, at some time or other, felt the want of an accurate, well written, concise, yet clear and reliable history of their own or some other state.

The want here indicated is now about being supplied; and, as the task of doing so is no light or superficial one, the publishers have given into the hands of the two gentlemen whose names appear in the title-page, the work of preparing a series of Cabinet Histories, embracing a volume for each state in the Union. Of their ability to perform this well, we need not speak. They are no strangers in the literary world. What they undertake the public may rest assured will be performed thoroughly, and that no sectarian, sectional, or party feelings will bias their judgment, or lead them to violate the integrity of history.

The importance of a series of state histories like those now commenced, can scarcely be estimated. Being condensed as carefully as accuracy and interest of narrative will permit, the size and price of the volumes will bring them within the reach of every family in the country, thus making them home-reading books for old and young. Each individual will, in consequence, become familiar, not only with the history of his own state, but with that of other states: —thus mutual interest will be re-awakened, and old bonds cemented in a firmer union.

In this series of CABINET HISTORIES, the authors, while presenting a concise but accurate narrative of the domestic policy of each state, will give greater prominence to the personal history of the people. The dangers which continually hovered around the early colonists; the stirring romance of a life passed fearlessly amid peril; the incidents of border warfare; the adventures of hardy pioneers; the keen watchfulness, the subtle surprise, the ruthless attack, and prompt retaliation—all these having had an important influence upon the formation of the American character, are to be freely recorded; while the progressive development of the citizens of each individual state from the rough forest-life of the earlier day to the polished condition of the present, will exhibit a picture of national expansion as instructing as it is interesting.

The size and style of the series will be uniform with the present volume. The authors, who have been for some time collecting and arranging materials, will furnish the succeeding volumes as rapidly as their careful preparation will warrant.

PREFACE.

As the first Anglo-Saxon colony in America, Virginia has always occupied an important historical position. But while detached portions of her early annals, full of romantic interest, have become familiar to all classes of persons, the connected narrative of the dangers and privations which attended her early settlement, and subsequent progress, has remained, for the most part, imperfectly known to the general reader.

To give this history in a compact form, neither coloured by prejudice nor distorted by party feeling, the present volume has been written. The materials for the work have been drawn from the most reliable sources, and it has been rendered as accurate as possible, by patient investigation and by a careful comparison of conflicting authorities.

CONTENTS.

CHAPTER I.

CHAPTER II.

CHAPTER III.

CHAPTER IV.

CHAPTER V.

CHAPTER VI.

CHAPTER VII.

CHAPTER VIII.

CHAPTER IX.

CHAPTER X.

CHAPTER XI.

CHAPTER XII.

CHAPTER XIII.

CHAPTER XIV.

CHAPTER XV.

CHAPTER XVI.

CHAPTER XVII.

CHAPTER XVIII.

CHAPTER XIX.

CHAPTER XX.

CHAPTER XXI.

CHAPTER XXII.

CHAPTER XXIII.

CHAPTER XXIV.

CHAPTER XXV.

CHAPTER XXVI.

HISTORY OF VIRGINIA.

CHAPTER I.

Early English explorers—John and Sebastian Cabot discover North America—Voyage of Sebastian Cabot—Voyage of Frobisher—Coligny founds a colony of Huguenots in Florida—The colonists massacred by the Spaniards—Retaliation of De Gourguis—First project of an English colony—Sir Walter Raleigh—Studies the art of war under Coligny—Returns to England—In favour with Queen Elizabeth—Obtains a patent to colonize America—Voyage of Sir Humphrey Gilbert—His shipwreck and loss at sea—Voyage of Amidas and Barlow—Description of the island of Wokokon in Florida—Kindness of the natives—Colony founded at Roanoke—Deserted—Voyage of Sir Richard Grenville—Second settlement of Roanoke—Mysterious disappearance of the colonists—Death of Raleigh—Voyage of Newport—Character of the immigrants—Captain John Smith—His romantic adventures in the old world.

No sooner was the great problem solved by Christopher Columbus, of immense and hitherto unknown regions beyond the Atlantic, than adventurers from the various maritime nations of Europe sought to profit by the discovery.

Among these, England, though not foremost in her explorations, was destined eventually to become the most distinguished.

On the 5th of March, 1496, John Cabot, a

Venetian merchant, residing at Bristol in England, obtained from Henry VII. a patent, empowering him and his three sons to make discoveries in the eastern, western, and northern seas, and to take possession of all the countries thus newly found, in the name of the King of England, and under the protection of his banner. Under this commission, John and Sebastian Cabot embarked for the west, and on the 24th of June, 1497, discovered the continent of North America, in latitude 56° north. This was some time before Columbus in his third voyage came in sight of the continent, and two years before Americus Vespucci sailed west of the Canaries.

It was from this expedition, by the Cabots, that England acquired the title to North America, which she afterward so successfully asserted.

In 1498, Sebastian Cabot ranged the same coast, from latitude 58° north to about 40° south, when finding himself growing short of provisions he returned to England.

Further maritime discoveries languished until 1576, when Martin Frobisher, under the patronage of the Earl of Warwick, fitted out a squadron for the purpose of attempting the discovery of a northwest passage to India. As he passed down the Thames, on the 8th of June, 1576, Queen Elizabeth waved her hand toward him in token of favour, and the admiral standing on the deck of his flag-ship, responded to the courteous recognition of his sovereign.

The fleet of Frobisher consisted of three vessels, one of which was soon lost in a storm. The commander of the second ship, becoming alarmed, put back for England, leaving the gallant admiral to pursue his voyage alone.

After enduring the most terrible hardships, Frobisher reached the coast of Labrador, entered the bay now known by his name, took possession of the country in the name of his sovereign, and gathering some stones and rubbish from the shore, which were supposed to be impregnated with gold, returned in safety to England.

Sixteen years previous to this exploit of Frobisher's, Admiral Coligny, chief of the Huguenot party in France, made two several attempts to found a colony far to the southward, on a portion of that vast region which was then known to Spanish adventurers as Florida. The first attempt ended disastrously, through dissensions among the colonists themselves. The fate of the second colony was more awful still. Spain maintained her right to Florida, and despatched one Pedro Melendez, a man of brutal ferocity and infamous character, with a large military and naval force, to break up the Huguenot settlement, and hold possession of the country.

No sooner had Melendez reached the coast of Florida, than, sailing north, he discovered the

French fleet lying at anchor, and in answer to a demand made by the French commander of his name and objects, he replied:

"I am Melendez of Spain, sent hither with strict orders from the king, to gibbet and behead all Protestants in these regions. The Frenchman who is a Catholic I will spare;—every heretic shall die."

The French, unprepared for action, cut their cables and fled. Melendez then returned to the harbour of St. Augustine, and after taking possession of the whole continent in the name of Philip II., marched overland against the Huguenot colony on the St. John's.

Fearing no danger, the unfortunate colonists were surprised and massacred in cold blood; men, women, and children, about two hundred in all! Of those who escaped into the woods, a part surrendered to the Spaniards, and were immediately murdered. Others succeeded in taking refuge on board a French vessel remaining in the harbour. Others again, who had escaped shipwreck on the coast, were soon discovered. Wasted by fatigues at sea, and half famished for want of food, they were invited by Melendez to rely on his mercy. They accordingly surrendered; and as they stepped on shore, their hands were tied before them, and they were thus driven to St. Augustine like sheep to a slaughter-house.

As they approached the fort, a signal was

given, the trumpet was sounded, and the Spaniards fell upon them. With the exception of a few Catholics, all were massacred; "not as Frenchmen, but as Lutherans."

About nine hundred, including those previously slain, were thus sacrificed on the altar of religious zeal.

The French government, itself perhaps even then meditating the terrible massacre of St. Bartholomew, heard of the outrage and listened to its horrid details with the most heartless indifference. Not even a protest was made. Retaliatory vengeance, however, fell upon the bloodthirsty Spaniards from a quarter whence it was perhaps the least expected.

Dominic de Gourguis, a native of Gascony, and a bold soldier, burning to avenge the blood of his slaughtered relatives, and soothe the cries of his persecuted brethren, fitted out three ships, manned by one hundred and fifty gallant men, and embarked for Florida. A favourable breeze soon wafted him thither; he landed immediately, and surprised two Spanish forts near the mouth of the St. John's. As terror magnified his numbers, and courage and revenge nerved his arm, he was enabled to get possession of the principal fort, near the spot where his relatives and friends had been previously massacred. Too weak to maintain his position, he weighed anchor immediately for Europe, having first hanged all his prisoners upon the trees, and placed over them this inscription:

"I do not this as unto Spaniards, but as unto traitors, robbers, and murderers."

It was to this region, so fearfully drenched with European blood, that the attention of an English gentleman was subsequently attracted as a fitting place of settlement for the first English colony.

About the time that the daring exploit of De Gourguis was creating a sensation in Europe, a young English gentleman left the university of Oxford, and passing over into France, prosecuted his studies in the art of war under the veteran Coligny. Being made familiar with the story of Spanish cruelty from the lips of those whose relatives had been thus wantonly murdered, and excited to a thirst for similar adventure by their glowing descriptions of the wonderful natural beauty of the land which had been thus savagely desecrated, Sir Walter Raleigh returned at length to England, filled with great projects by which he might win renown to himself and glory to his country. His flattering and chivalrous gallantry in spreading his rich cloak before the feet of his sovereign, so that she might pass a muddy space unsoiled, his handsome person, and the varied charms of his conversation, very soon commended him to the favourable regard of the vainest but ablest of English queens. Any project which would check the spread of Spanish colonies over a continent she claimed by right of Cabot's discovery, could not be otherwise than pleasing to her, who at Tilbury Fort subsequently dared the landing of the formidable Armada, and cheered the spirits of her soldiers by proclaiming that, "though she had the form of a woman, she had the heart of a king, ay, and of a king of England too."

Under her auspices, accordingly, in 1583, Sir Walter Raleigh equipped a fleet at his own expense. The command he gave to his step-brother, Sir Humphrey Gilbert, who, on his departure, received from Elizabeth a golden anchor, guided by a lady, as a token of her regard. Gilbert first sailed for Newfoundland. Entering the harbour of St. John, he took possession of the country, in the name of his sovereign, with all the formalities then customary on such occasions. After freighting his largest ship, in secret, with the same kind of mineral which had attracted Frobisher at an earlier day, Gilbert sailed in a southern direction along the coast on a voyage of exploration. His largest ship was wrecked by the carelessness of its crew, and nearly a hundred men, with all the mineral, was lost. Sir Humphrey himself had embarked on board the Squirrel, a pinnace of ten tons, in order to approach nearer to the coast, ascertain its bearings, and explore its harbours; and, being unwilling to forsake the little company with whom he had encountered so many storms, he attempted, in this frail bark, scarcely superior to the long-boat of a merchantman, to cross the vast Atlantic.

The sea was rough, the winds high, and the oldest mariners had rarely witnessed the like. The little bark bore up manfully for a while, but was too small to dare the ocean at that season of the year; and, when last seen, Sir Humphrey Gilbert was sitting abaft, with a book in his hand, crying out to those in another vessel that followed in his wake, "We are as near to heaven by sea as by land." The same night, a little before twelve o'clock, the lights of the Squirrel suddenly disappeared, and neither vessel nor crew were heard of more.

Raleigh, having determined to secure, at all events, those delightful regions to England, from which the French Protestants had been expelled, was neither disheartened by the fate of his step-brother, nor appalled by the magnitude of the undertaking. He immediately set on foot another expedition, and associating with him Sir Richard Grenville, and sundry other gentlemen and merchants, equipped two ships, which were placed under the command of Captain Philip Amidas and Captain Barlow, who sailed from the Thames on the 27th day of April, 1584, taking the southerly route by the Canaries and the West Indies.

On the 2d of July they fell in with the coast of Florida in shoal water, where they were greeted with a "most delicate sweet smell, though they saw no land," which before long they spied, and coasted along it for a hundred and twenty miles without finding any harbour.

The first that appeared they entered with much difficulty, and anchored. Then returning thanks to God, they landed, and took possession in the queen's name.

They found their landing-place sandy and low, but so full of grapes that the very surge of the sea sometimes overflowed them; of which they found such plenty in all places, both in the sand, the green soil, and the hills, as in the plains; as well on every little shrub, as also climbing toward the top of high cedars, that they thought there was not in the world a like abundance. The place where they landed proved to be an island called Wokokon.

For three days after their arrival, they saw none of the inhabitants. On the third day three of them appeared in a little boat, one of whom, suffering himself to be taken without resistance, came boldly on board the vessel, and was dismissed with presents, with which he seemed well pleased.

The next day came many boats, and in one of them the king's brother with forty or fifty men. His name was Grangranameo: they called their king *Wingina*, and their country *Wingandacoa.*

Leaving his boats at a short distance from the ships, he came with his train to the point, where, spreading a mat, he sat down.

Though the strangers came to him armed, he evinced no fear or distrust, stroking his head and breast and theirs also with his hand in sign of peace and friendship. He then addressed them with a long speech, and accepted the presents offered to him. He was highly regarded by his people, for all stood in silence but four, on whom presents were also bestowed, but he took them away, and made signs to indicate that every thing belonged to him.

The king himself was absent, in consequence of wounds received in a recent battle.

Grangranameo repeated his visits, came on board the ships with confidence, and brought with him his wife and children. They were of mean stature, but well-favoured and bashful. She wore a long coat of dressed deer-skin prettily fringed, and about her forehead a band of white coral. In her ears were strings of pearls hanging down to her middle, of the size of large peas; the rest of the women had pendants of copper, and the chiefs, or nobles, five or six in each ear. The apparel of Grangranameo was similar to that of his wife, only the women wore their hair long on both sides, and the men on one. Their hair was black, but there were seen children having it of a light copper color.

On one of their visits, Grangranameo took a great fancy for a pewter dish, which so pleased him that he gave twenty deer-skins for it, and hung it about his neck in great pride. For a copper kettle he gave fifty deer-skins. For an armour he would have given a bag of pearls; but the English affected an indifference to their value, in order to ascertain the place from whence they were derived. He was just to his promise, always came true to his appointed time, and daily sent presents of game and fruits.

From thence a party proceeded in exploring the neighbouring coast, and landed at the island of Roanoke, where ultimately the location of a colony was fixed.

In 1586, another expedition was undertaken, under the command of Grenville, at the expense of a company formed for the support of the colony, but with the most unfortunate results; and Sir Francis Drake, having sailed along the coast of Virginia, was prevailed upon by the colonists to take them back to England.

Efforts were renewed in 1587, by Sir Walter Raleigh and Sir Richard Grenville, for the re-establishment of the colony, and another vessel prepared, in which men with their wives and families embarked. The company was now cheered for the first time with the presence of women. They carried also implements of husbandry, indications of future industry.

Having arrived on the coast of North Carolina in July, 1587, they repaired immediately to the island of Roanoke. Soon after their landing, difficulties thickened. A detachment of English, seeing a party of Indians sitting fearlessly around their fires at night, and supposing they were enemies, took them by surprise, and before their error was detected, a large portion of the number were cruelly massacred. The Indians became hostile, and the immigrants gloomy and discontented. They urged the governor, John White, to return to England for reinforcements and supplies. Before his return, his daughter, who had been married to Ananias Dare, one of the magistrates of the colony, gave birth to an infant, which, being the first child born of English parents in North America, was christened "Virginia," from the place of its birth.

By the generosity of Raleigh, White was despatched with supplies in two vessels. Preferring, however, a gainful rather than a safe voyage, he departed from his course in pursuit of prizes; fell in with a Spanish man-of-war, and was boarded, and rifled of all he had.

This delay proved fatal to the colony. Two years elapsed before White was enabled to return. When he reached Roanoke, he found the island deserted; and with the exception of the word CROATAN, carved in large Roman letters upon one of the posts of the palisades, there was no indication of how or in what manner the unfortunate colonists had disappeared. Several expeditions were subsequently fitted out for their discovery; but the manner of their fate remains a mystery to this day.

The misfortunes which afterward befell the brave and gallant Sir Walter Raleigh are well known to all students of English history. He was the first and noblest of English adventurers. His efforts at colonization, in which he expended from his own private fortune forty thousand pounds, equal at the present time to nearly a million of dollars, were stimulated as much by his zeal for the honour of his sovereign as for his own personal aggrandizement. The conquest of Cadiz and the capture of Fayal would alone have established his military fame. Implicated in the civil dissensions of his country, while languishing in a prison he composed a history of the world. Broken-hearted and impoverished, his sentence, originally unjust, which had slumbered for fifteen years, was revived by the timid and pedantic tyrant James I., under whose warrant he was finally beheaded before the Tower of London.

For the space of nearly twenty years succeeding the disappearance of the colony at Roanoke, no further attempt to settle any portion of the American continent was made by the English people.

At length the spirit of adventure was again

revived; the minds of many wealthy and influential persons were directed once more to Virginia, and two rival companies sought and obtained patents from James I., who wrote with his own hand many of the regulations by which the settlements were to be governed.

Twelve degrees of latitude were set apart on the American coast, from Cape Fear to Halifax, for the purposes of colonization. The London company were to occupy the regions between the thirty-fourth and thirty-eighth degrees of latitude; that is, from Cape Fear to the southern limit of Maryland: the Plymouth company, between the forty-first and forty-fifth degrees of latitude. The intermediate space was left open to the competition of both.

The conditions of the tenure were homage and rent. The latter to consist of one-fifth of the net produce of gold and silver, and one-fifteenth of copper. The superintendence of the whole colonial system was confided to a council in England, and the local administration to a council residing within its limits. The king reserved to himself the exclusive right to appoint the members of the superior council, and an almost equal control over the councils to be established in the colonies. To the immigrants nothing was given, not even the right of self-government. They were subjected to the ordinances of a commercial corporation, of which they could not be members;

to the dominion of a domestic council, in the appointment of which they had no choice; to the control of a superior council in England, which had no sympathy with their rights; and, finally, to the arbitrary legislation of the sovereign.

On the 19th of December, 1606, three ships, freighted by the London adventurers, set sail from Blackwall, in England. One hundred colonists accompanied the expedition, the command of which was intrusted to Captain Newport, an experienced mariner. Of these colonists more than one-half were gentlemen by birth and education; and, of course, from previous habits, the least fitted for the purposes of a new settlement. Among these latter, however, were a few whose inherent energy of character speedily rendered them conspicuous both for conduct and enterprise. The most remarkable of all, both on account of his previous adventures, and the romantic incidents connected with his subsequent history, was Captain John Smith. Although his age did not at this time much exceed thirty years, he had already acquired a fame for noble daring, and a character for singular exploits, which, were they not so well authenticated, would in this age be esteemed as little less than fabulous.

Bred to the profession of a soldier, his first effort in arms was in the Low Countries, where he fought for the independence of Holland. From thence he travelled through France, visited

Egypt, and returned to Italy. Having there heard of an hereditary warfare between the Christian and the Moor on the borders of Hungary, he repaired thither, and in three successive combats, with as many infidel champions, came off victorious. He thus gained the favour of Sigismund, the unfortunate Prince of Transylvania, by whom he was commissioned as a captain in the army of Christendom.

Overpowered by numbers, in a sudden skirmish with the Moslems among the glens of Wallachia, he was severely wounded, and left for dead upon the field. He was soon after carried to Constantinople, as a prisoner of war, and sold in its market for a slave.

The lady of his master, taking pity on his sufferings, and admiring his bravery, sent him to her friend in the Crimea, intending from thence to restore him to freedom. Contrary, however, to her commands, he was there subjected to the severest hardships, against which his indignant spirit rebelled. Rising upon his task-master, whom he slew in the struggle, he mounted a horse and escaped into Russia. Travelling across that country on foot to Transylvania, he bade adieu to his companions, and resolved to return to England.

Hearing, however, on his journey thither, of civil wars raging in Northern Africa, he hastened to Morocco in search of new adventures, and proceeded thence to his own country, where he arrived some short time previous to the period when Newport and others were about to sail for Virginia. Partaking of their excitement, at the instance of Captain Gosnold, he embarked with them, and was destined at a future day to render his name, already famous in the old world, immortal in the new.

CHAPTER II.

Jamestown—Description of site selected for settlement—Gathering of the colonists—Charges preferred against Captain John Smith—His innocence substantiated—Wingfield fined—Exploration of James River—Village of Powhattan—Description of an Indian village—Its place of games—Its sacred fire—Sepulchre of the chiefs—Their idol Kiwasa—Construction of their wigwams—Internal arrangement—Regal state of Powhattan—His wives—Obedience of his subjects—His places of residence—Orapakes—Description of Powhattan's dwelling—Character of Powhattan.

About fifty miles from the mouth of James River, and forming a part of its left bank, as the stream flows, there is a remarkable tongue of land, jutting well out into the river, which is navigable up to this point for ships of the largest burden. The lower shoulder of this peninsula is intersected by a creek, which, curving sharply across it, nearly cuts it off from the main land. It was this peninsula which the adventurers selected as the site for their colony, and named it Jamestown.

The reasons which influenced the council in their selection, were, probably, its capabilities of defence from the natives, and its easy access from the ocean. In most other respects the situation thus deliberately chosen was unfavourable. The banks were low, and the place, by reason of marshes in its immediate vicinity, peculiarly unhealthy to persons whose constitutions had been formed in the less genial, but more invigorating climate of England. It has long since been deserted for more attractive localities, and all the indications that now remain of its early settlement are the venerable ruins of an old brick church, and a few half obliterated graves within whose narrow limits the ashes of the first adventurers repose.

Let us now take a retrospective glance at the busy scene which exhibited itself to the eyes of the wondering savages on the 13th of May, 1607, a day to be remembered for ever in the annals of the American nation.

Close in to the bank, for the depth of water admits of this proximity, are moored three vessels, the largest of which is not superior to the common bay craft which now navigate its river. Two of these, Newport's ship of one hundred tons, and another of forty, after disembarking the immigrants and unloading the stores, are to return to England freighted with such articles as the country will immediately yield. The third, a pinnace of twenty tons, is to remain in Virginia for the use of the colonists.

The latter are already disembarked, and with a vigour which will soon suffer abatement, are busily employed in felling timber, defending their provisions from the chances of the weather, and securing their arms in dry vats. In among the tall and stately trees, tents, the first temporary habitations of the settlers, are seen whitely gleaming. After a while the men break from their work, and congregating together, listen, beneath the overarching greenery of the sylvan wilderness, to an oration from Mr. Wingfield, who has been appointed governor, explaining the reason why Captain Smith—though so nominated in England—is not admitted as one of the council.

Even while on shipboard, the superiority of the young man Smith to the rest of his companions had so manifested itself as to excite the base fears and malignant envy of a few well-conditioned, but feeble-spirited men, who were ambitious of supreme rule in the new land to which they were then bound.

During the voyage he had been suddenly seized and imprisoned, and upon the landing of the colonists, he was charged by Wingfield, who appears to have been his principal enemy, with an intention of usurping the government, murdering the council, and making himself king.

Fearing to bring a charge of so heinous a nature to open proof, Wingfield and his confederates affected, from a merciful disposition, to refrain from trying their prisoner in the colony for a crime which, if substantiated, would involve the taking of his life, and strenuously insisted upon sending him back to England, to undergo merely the milder censure of the superior council.

These efforts Smith as strongly resented. He demanded to be confronted with the unknown witnesses of his accusers; and as the public voice sympathized with the justness of his demand, Wingfield was compelled to acquiesce. After many shifts and delays, the trial was commenced; the result of which was, that all the company saw through the malice of Smith's enemies: those suborned to accuse him, accused their employers of subornation; Wingfield incurred the general hatred of the colony, and was mulcted in a fine of two hundred pounds, as a compensation to Smith for his sufferings. This fine, the latter immediately made over to the public store for the general use of the immigrants.

By the exhortations of Mr. Hunt, a pious clergyman, who was much beloved by the colonists, a reconciliation took place soon afterward between Smith and his adversaries, and Smith was admitted a member of the council. The next day all received the communion. Between energy and uprightness on the one hand, and weakness and malignity on the other, no permanent harmony was to be expected.

Such was the first episode which distinguished the settlement of Jamestown; others of a more fearful character were soon to follow.

In the mean while, however, and pending the day set apart for his trial, Smith was permitted to accompany Newport in the pinnace to discover the head of the river. Cautiously exploring the creeks and inlets on their way, they reached on the sixth day a village of twelve houses or wigwams, within a mile of the falls of James River, and a little below where the town of Richmond now stands.

This village, pleasantly situated on a hill, with three fertile isles before it, and surrounded by a corn-field, was called Powhattan. The name of its chief in the Indian tongue was Wahunsanocock. He was called by the English Powhattan, from the chief seat and metropolis of his hereditary dominion; and, by way of eminence, the emperor.

When the English landed in Virginia, its native population was broken up into a number of petty tribes, numbering some eight thousand souls, generally at war with each other, and yet loosely united into a sort of confederacy, of which Wahunsanocock, or Powhattan, as he was subsequently called, was the acknowledged chief.

In the times of the first European settlers, the construction of the wigwams of the natives and the arrangement of their towns differed very materially from those of their descendants at the present day.

Most of the Indian villages in Virginia, were enclosed by a palisade of strong upright poles, firmly planted in the ground near to each other, and penetrated only by a single narrow entrance. Within and around this circular area, the houses were disposed, leaving a clear open space in the centre. Upon some part of this open space was a smaller circle, enclosed by six or seven posts, somewhat higher than a man, rudely carved with human faces of a hideous or grotesque character. Here it was, at certain seasons of the year, they assembled with their neighbours to celebrate their solemn feasts with songs and dances. On the opposite side from this place, set apart for the purposes of festivity, were as many other posts set low in the ground, in the midst of which their sacred fire was kept always burning. Near to the latter was the sepulchre of their chiefs, an oblong building with a semicircular roof, similar in appearance without to the better class of dwellings. Internally the arrangements were very different. Entering this gloomy structure, the first thing that the eye rested upon was a raised platform, some nine or ten feet in height, on which, side by side in extended rows, lay the dead bodies of their chiefs, whose bowels and fleshy parts had been removed, dried, and enclosed in boxes, at the feet of the skeletons, over which the skin was carefully replaced. Beneath this horrible platform was the habitation of a priest, whose duty was, night and day, to mutter prayers and watch the dead. At the side above, on a raised seat overlooking the bodies, was placed their idol Kiwasa, a roughly carved figure about four feet high, with its face painted red, its breast white, and the rest of its body black, except the legs, which were variegated with white. Folds of delicately dressed deer-skin encircled the loins, and around the neck were suspended loose necklaces of white beads, mixed with larger ones of copper.

The wigwams, or houses, were constructed of light saplings, bent over to meet each other at the top in the form of an arbour, the light ribs being firmly strengthened by transverse poles securely fastened. Over this frame was thrown a close covering of mats made of reeds, and impervious to the weather. Around the interior walls ran a slight narrow staging, raised from the ground a foot or more; on this they slept, covered with mats or skins, the head of one slumberer touching the feet of another. Some of these wigwams were a hundred feet in length, and exhibited a slight increase in civilization by being divided into separate compartments, the best constructed containing four or five.

Primitive, however, as was the condition of his subjects, Powhattan exacted from them as many ceremonial observances as were then or are now paid to the potentates of more enlightened countries. He kept about his person from forty to fifty men. Every night four sentinels were stationed at the four corners of his dwelling, and at each half hour one of his body-guard made a signal to the four sentinels. He kept as many wives as he thought proper. When the English saw him at home reclining on his couch, or platform, there was always one sitting at his head and another at his feet; and when he sat, two of them seated themselves on either side of him. At his meals, one of them brought him a wooden platter in which to wash his hands before and after eating, while another attended him with a bunch of feathers for a towel; some were the daughters, and some had been the wives, of distinguished rivals and enemies conquered in battle. When he became weary of them, he transferred them as presents to his favourite warriors.

So imposing was the authority he exercised over his rude followers, that when he spoke, they obeyed him as a king, and esteemed him with a reverence allied to divinity. What he commanded, they immediately performed; they presented at his feet whatever he directed to be brought, and at the least frown of his brow the boldest of them would tremble with fear.

In one particular aspect, Powhattan possessed a decided advantage over his brother monarchs in Europe; he could make his own robes, shoes, bows, arrows, and pots, besides planting his corn for exercise, and hunting deer for amusement. Like other emperors, Powhattan had as many as three or four places of residence. One of these was at Werowocomoco, on the Pamunky River, a little in the rear and below Jamestown. Its proximity to the English settlements soon caused him to abandon the latter for his royal house at Orapakes, somewhere near the head waters of the Chickahominy, as rendering him less likely to be disturbed by those whom he could not but consider as disagreeable neighbours.

During the last years of his life, he secluded himself at Orapakes almost entirely. Here were deposited his royalties and his revenue, skins, copper, beads and paint, bows and arrows, targets and clubs. The house itself was of great length. Four rudely graven images of wood were stationed at the four corners—one representing a dragon, the second a bear, the third a panther, and the fourth a gigantic man; all made "evil favouredly," according to the best workmanship of the natives. Such was the regal and barbarous state in which lived the Emperor Powhattan, the father of the gentle princess Pocahontas, whose tender and graceful deeds will shortly appear on the pages of this history.

Shrewd and politic, this ancient monarch of the wilderness quietly retreated to a distance from the new comers, whose singular and unexpected advent he could not but view with alarm, though he prudently concealed his fears. Remoteness and forbearance he felt to be his best safeguard; and when some of his subjects complained at the intrusion of the strangers, he wisely checked their rising anger by calmly replying: "That the strangers did not hurt them; they only took a little of their waste land."

Whether, if the first settlers had conformed strictly to the orders from England, by which kindness to the savages was enjoined, they could have dwelt in peace and friendship with their sylvan neighbours, is a problem which involves some difficulty in its solution. Captain Smith subsequently answered the question in his own sharp cutting way. He evidently regarded the nature of the Indian as similar to that of the Egyptian Arab, whose love for an individual is in proportion to the fear with which he inspires him; and certainly, if the reverence accorded to that gallant martialist by his savage antagonists be considered as any evidence of their esteem, it must be acknowledged that he made his proposition good.

It was reserved for William Penn to solve the problem in a different and far more merciful way. In forming our judgment, however, it must be recollected that Penn met the Indians under auspices infinitely more favourable to the success of his mission. The English were then numerous in the land, their strength was known and tested, their courage justly feared, and the savages could, at that time, have entertained no very sanguine hopes of success in the event of rising to attempt the expulsion of the intruders.

And yet, notwithstanding these arguments, we incline to the belief that Penn was right, and that the interpretation of the bolder and elder adventurer was erroneous.

CHAPTER III.

Description of the colonists—Gentlemen idlers—Noticeable men—Mr. Hunt—Mr. George Percy—Captain Bartholomew Gosnold—His death—Portrait of Captain John Smith—Careless security of the colonists—Attacked by the Indians—Fort built and palisadoed—Newport leaves for England—Famine and sickness in the colony—Selfishness of Wingfield—Attempts to escape from the colony—Deposed—Sufferings of the settlers—Their providential deliverance—Energy of Smith—Explores the country for provisions—Conspiracy of Wingfield and Kendall—Death of Kendall—Abundance in the colony.

WHILE Smith and his companions were on their return voyage from the royal village of Powhattan, an event occurred at Jamestown which seriously endangered the permanence of the settlement.

But before we narrate the incidents connected with this affair, it may, perhaps, be as well to give a passing glance at the colonists themselves.

We have already stated that more than one-half of those who were destined to form the nucleus of a great and powerful nation were gentlemen by birth and education. But, if by this it should be understood that the majority of them were men of wealth and standing in their own land, the conclusion would be very far from correct. On the contrary, at least four-fifths of those who styled themselves gentlemen, and by the courtesy of their companions were acknowledged as such, were starveling gallants, thriftless younger sons, reckless tavern-haunting vagabonds, sent by their friends to Virginia, to escape a worse fate at home;—a part of that floating scum which always rises in the midst of a dense population.

These idle do-nothings in taffeta rags, with roses in their shoes, and swaling feathers in their hats, swaggered about among the more industrious settlers, too proud to soil their delicate hands with labour, but always ready to claim their full share of the contents of the common kettle.

It was of these gentlemen, impoverished in spirit and fortune,—these rakes and libertines, men more fitted to corrupt, than to found a commonwealth,—that Captain Smith, at a later day, indignantly wrote to the council in London, saying: "I entreat you, when you send next, to send thirty carpenters, husbandmen, gardeners, fishermen, blacksmiths, masons, and diggers-up of trees' roots, rather than a thousand such as we have."

But while the vitality of the infant colony was thus hampered by the dead weight of these hangers-on, there yet remained a few noticeable men, of the better class, who constantly endeavoured, both by precept and example, to sustain its failing energies.

First among these, in respect to his walk and calling, must be mentioned the good clergyman, Mr. Hunt. Those who have studied to any purpose the contemporaneous chronicles of the early struggles in Virginia, cannot fail to recall the mild, pale, patient face of this worthiest and most beloved of men,—he who by his good doctrines and exhortations so often succeeded in soothing the angry, checking the unruly, and reconciling those who were at enmity with each other.

Another of the immigrants was Mr. George Percy, a brother of the Earl of Northumberland, who in 1611 received from the hands of Lord De la Warre the government of the colony, and is worthily praised by him as a gentleman of honour and resolution.

Among the more remarkable of the immigrants, might also have been seen the weather-beaten form of Captain Bartholomew Gosnold, an elderly mariner, who, having previously made several voyages along the coast of America, became one of the most enthusiastic and efficient promoters of the enterprise which led to its settlement. The honest old seaman did not live long enough to witness the success of the scheme he had so generously fostered. Within a few months after his landing upon the peninsula of Jamestown, there was an open grave in the little churchyard of the colony, and around it stood many haggard and half-famished mourners, while the voice of good Mr. Hunt, in accents mournful yet solemn, murmured those awfully sublime words which form the grandest service for the dead in any known tongue.

But the man of men, he who, though but of medium stature, was elevated by his deeds a full head and shoulders above his companions, was young Captain John Smith. His portrait yet remains for the satisfaction of those curious in such matters. A sturdy, athletic figure, clad in leathern doublet and trunk hose, gathered loosely at the knee; low-quartered shoes beneath, and on his head a broad-leaved beaver: the face, indicative of the man, bearded like the pard, swarthy, and of a leonine aspect.

Returning to Jamestown, we shall find, that during the absence of Smith and his companions—an absence extended to some eight or ten days—but little was done by the colonists.

Wingfield, the governor, as feeble and vacillating as he had heretofore proved himself malicious, was but ill calculated to direct and govern as unruly a set of spirits as were ever associated together, even in a tavern haunt of Alsatia. Newport was with Smith, and though there yet remained behind four gentlemen of the council only, Kendall and good old Captain Gosnold laboured to preserve order and diligence, with such energy as was in them.

In the mean time, the Indians, with a great

show of friendship, visited the settlers daily, bringing with them many presents of game and fish, in order to render their coming as welcome as possible. Admitted thus freely into the heart of the encampment, and mingling without restraint with both workmen and idlers, the quick-eyed savages soon observed that every man was unarmed; and that the only protection from assault was a light semicircular breastwork, formed of the boughs of trees, which had been thrown up by the diligence of Captain Kendall.

This state of careless security, without doubt, instigated the Indians, already jealous of their lands being thus unceremoniously seized, to attempt, by a sudden attack, either the extermination or expulsion of the strange intruders.

Accordingly, the day before the return of Smith from Powhattan, and while the settlers were scattered in various parts of the encampment, they were surprised by the sudden hurtling of a cloud of arrows, followed by the shrill war-whoop of the savages. Seventeen men fell wounded, and a boy was slain; the remainder of the colonists rushed with confused outcries towards the ships, followed by their swarthy and exulting foes. Fortunately, a quick hand from one of the ships fired a cross-bar shot at the pursuers, which, striking down a bough of a tree among them, caused them to retire as precipitately as they had at first advanced.

Thus terribly admonished, Wingfield no longer opposed the arming of the settlers. All other labour was suspended until a strong fort could be erected and palisadoed; and, when this was accomplished, Newport sailed for England, leaving the colonists to their own resources.

These resources were soon found to be meagre enough. The ships had scarcely been gone ten days before almost every man in the colony was reduced to a state of extreme weakness, either from want of food, or from the relaxing character of the climate.

The means of subsistence were indeed alarmingly scanty. Half a pint of wheat, and as much barley, boiled in water, constituted each man's daily allowance, and these, having "fried" some twenty-six weeks in the ship's hold, contained as many worms as grains. "Had we been as free from sins as from gluttony and drunkenness," writes Smith, "we might have been canonized as saints."

But in the midst of this dreadful famine and sickness, and while his despairing people were fast sinking around him, Wingfield the governor took excellent care that his own personal comfort should suffer as little abatement as possible, by engrossing to his private use the beef, wine, oatmeal, and eggs, remaining in the public store.

Finding, at length, the long suppressed indignation of the colonists was roused against him, he attempted to add treachery to selfishness. He conspired with some few others, among whom perhaps Captain Kendall was one, to seize the pinnace, and by thus cutting off the last hope of escape to the settlers, leave them to their fate. What that fate would have been, it is not difficult to imagine.

Fortunately, the design was discovered, and as promptly frustrated. Wingfield and Kendall were deposed from their offices, and Ratcliffe elected governor.

Harassed continually by the savages, and weakened by labour, famine, and disease, within four months, or between May and September, one-half of the colonists died; while the remaining fifty, less happy than those who had gone before, barely managed to sustain life from day to day, by the sturgeon and crabs, which for their constant wants, the river too scantily afforded.

At length, when all their provision was gone, when even sturgeon was no longer to be had, and while they were hourly expecting to fall beneath the fury of the savages, by what Smith rightly ascribes to the interposition of an overwatching Providence, a remarkable circumstance took place. Those very savages, hitherto so watchful and unrelenting, filled with pity for the sufferings of which they had been so long hostile witnesses, brought to the poor, famished, and despairing settlers so great an abundance of fruit and provisions, that health was speedily restored, and no man any longer wanted for food.

By the death of Captain Gosnold and the deposition of Wingfield and Kendall, the government of the colony fell into the hands of three persons only; Ratcliffe, the governor, and Martin, and Smith, of the council. The two former, being men of weak judgment in danger, and little industry in peace, soon committed the management of affairs abroad into the hands of their more energetic associate.

The happy consequence of this surrender of power to the only man capable of exercising it to the best advantage, was soon made clearly apparent. Placing himself at the head of the work to be performed, Smith set some to build houses, some to mow and collect reeds, and others to thatch; always selecting the severest labour for himself; so that, in a short time, he had provided the most of his companions with comfortable dwellings, neglecting any for his own use. When this was done, finding the provisions brought in by the savages falling short, he took the pinnace, and made several journeys to Kecoughtan and the river Chickahominy, where he succeeded in obtaining supplies of corn.

But what he carefully provided, the rest as carelessly spent; and while he was absent, Wingfield and Kendall, then living in disgrace, enticed some sailors and others to join them in seizing the pinnace, with the intention of deserting the colony and sailing for England. The conspiracy was very near being successful; just as they were in the act of taking their departure, Smith unexpectedly returned, and bringing his cannon to bear upon the receding vessel, compelled the conspirators either to stay, or sink. They chose to haul to, and surrender, but not until after Captain Kendall had fallen in the action. A little while subsequent to this, another project was formed by Governor Ratcliffe and Captain Archer to obtain the pinnace, and abandon the country. This plot was also discovered, and as promptly suppressed by Smith. And now, the winter approaching, the rivers became so covered with wild fowl that they daily feasted. What with good bread, vegetables, fish, and various sorts of game, as fat as they could eat them, even the most froward and dissatisfied among them became perfectly reconciled to the country, and no longer desired to leave it.

CHAPTER IV.

Smith's superior abilities create envy—He explores the Chickahominy River to its source—Three of his men slain by the Indians—Smith taken prisoner—Led in procession to Orapakes—Gratitude of a savage—Smith carried in triumph through various tribes—Reaches Pamunkey—Singular conjurations of the medicine-men—Is taken to Werowocomoco—Regal state of Powhattan—Smith sentenced to death—Rescued by Pocahontas—His release—Returns to Jamestown—Represses the malcontents—They plot his death—His summary proceedings.

The superior talents of Captain Smith had by this time made themselves so manifest, that in proportion to the esteem in which he was held by the generality of the people, he was hated by the malcontents whose evil designs he had so signally thwarted.

Even the governor and Captain Martin, finding their official station but lightly regarded, began to look upon their more vigorous associate with an evil eye. Being determined to rid themselves of his presence in the settlement as much as possible, they taunted Smith with not having discovered the head of Chickahominy River, and charged him with dilatoriness. The fiery and impetuous soldier, who could but ill brook an accusation of this kind, immediately set sail on his voyage of exploration, although the season was so far advanced as to make the adventure both dangerous and uncertain.

Entering the river, he sailed toward its source, until its manifold obstructions prevented his barge from proceeding any farther. Leaving his little vessel at the distance of a bow-shot from the shore, after giving strict orders to his crew not to land, but to await his return, he entered a small canoe, and with two Englishmen and a couple of Indian guides, penetrated twenty miles higher, until he reached the marshes which were formed at the head of the river.

He was scarcely out of sight of the barge, before the men, disobeying his commands, went ashore and were surprised by the Indians, who had been directed by Opechancanough, the brother of Powhattan, to watch their motions. One man, George Cassen, was captured, and after being interrogated as to the direction taken by Captain Smith, was put to death. The rest escaped with difficulty to the barge.

The Indians now started in pursuit of Smith, killed the two men he had left in charge of his canoe, and at length discovered the captain himself. Although surrounded by two hundred savages, Smith, unconscious of the fate which had befallen his companions, resolved to attempt a retreat towards his canoe. Binding the Indian guide to his arm as a shield against the arrows of his foes, he kept up a running fire upon them, killed three, and wounded many others. During this time, however, Smith himself had not escaped wholly unscathed. One arrow had already pierced his thigh, and several penetrated his clothes; but his courage was so well appreciated, and the dread of his fire-arms was so great, that it is probable he might even then have succeeded in making good his escape, if, while retiring with his face toward his foes, he had not fallen into a marshy creek. Notwithstanding he was thus most effectually disabled, the Indians were afraid to approach him until, being nearly dead with cold, he threw away his arms.

Drawing him from the creek, they led him toward his canoe, where the first sight that met his eyes was the dead bodies of his two men, shot full of arrows, and lying by the fire they had lighted; the embers of which were still glowing.

After suffering the Indians to chafe his benumbed limbs until the blood once more circulated freely, Smith demanded to be shown their chief.

As soon as Opechancanough presented himself, the young soldier drew from his pocket a round ivory double compass dial, and gave it to his captor. The savages immediately gathered round the singular piece of mechanism, and were greatly astonished at the incessant motion of the needle, which they could see so plainly, and yet not touch, because of the glass by which it was covered. But when Smith demonstrated, by means of that little instrument, the roundness of the earth and skies, the spherical character of the sun, moon, and stars, and many other suchlike mysteries, they were filled with awe and admiration.

If, however, the bold young soldier sought by this means to ingratiate himself with the savages and so win them over to his release, he was doomed to a bitter disappointment. Within an hour afterward they suddenly pinioned his arms, and tying him to a tree, as many as could stand about him bent their bows, and were in the act of despatching him, when Opechancanough, holding up the compass in his hand, commanded them to desist.

He was then led in triumphant procession, under a strong guard, to the town of Orapakes. As he approached it, all the women and children came out to gaze at the great warrior, whose renown had already preceded him.

On entering the town the procession halted. The Indians, then forming a ring, danced wildly about their prisoner, accompanying their uncouth gestures with songs and ear-piercing yells.

All this while Smith and Opechancanough stood in the midst guarded. When the dances were ended, Opechancanough conducted his prisoner to a long house, covered with mats, where he was placed under the protection of some thirty or forty warriors, every one with his head and shoulders painted of a bright scarlet colour, and all of them bearing bows in their hands, a quiver of arrows and a club slung at their backs, and on the arm of each, by way of vambrace, a fox, or otter's skin.

Food was soon afterward set before him in quantities sufficient for twenty men, and at midnight another and equally abundant supply was brought in. What he did not eat was put into baskets and slung to the rafters above his head. No one was suffered to partake of the meal with him.

The next morning fresh provisions were brought, and in such profusion, that Smith conjectured the design of the savages was to fatten, and then eat him. Even in this desperate strait, he met with an instance of gratitude which is well worthy of record.

Observing him to shiver with the cold, an Indian by the name of Macassater stript himself of his own robe and gave it to Smith, in requital for some beads and other toys which the latter had presented him on his first arrival in Virginia.

The second day of his imprisonment, an Indian, in revenge for the loss of his son, who then lay mortally wounded, attempted to murder Smith, but his purpose was prevented by the timely interposition of the guards.

It is an evidence of their credulous belief in the almost supernatural power of their prisoner, that they conducted him to the couch of the dying man, with the hope of his being yet able to restore him to health. With that quickness of perception which so eminently marked the character of the man, Smith immediately profited by the opportunity. He told them, that at Jamestown he had a water that would do it, if they would permit him to go there for it; this, however, they shrewdly declined. On the contrary, they made great preparations for an assault upon the settlement, and sought the advice of their prisoner. As an inducement to assist them, they offered him life, liberty, and land. The wily soldier neither accepted nor refused, but, temporizing with them, obtained with great difficulty permission to send messengers to the fort, bearing his table-book, ostensibly for the purpose of obtaining certain things for his own use, but in reality with a view to inform the colonists of his situation, and place them on their guard against surprise.

Notwithstanding the way was long, and the weather bitter cold, the messengers performed their journey and returned to Orapakes within three days, wondering greatly by what strange conjurations it was that a small piece of white paper could be made to talk.

But if this, to them, singular faculty of conveying his thoughts to a distance by means of certain arbitrary characters, led them to regard their prisoner with increased awe, it did not prevent them from rejoicing still more heartily at the knowledge that so dangerous a man was a captive in their hands.

Triumphantly, and with songs and dances, they led him captive through the chief towns of the surrounding tribes, and thence back again to the king's habitation at Pamunkey.

At this place a consultation appears to have been held among the chief priests and medicine-men of the various tribes. The subject of their deliberations was one of great gravity and moment. It was to ascertain whether the captive white warrior, whose marvellous doings challenged alike the admiration and the fears of the savages, was possessed of evil intentions toward them.

It was a knotty problem, the solution of which could only be obtained by fearful conjurations, and the exercise of their best skill in art magic.

Accordingly, one morning, a great fire was made in one of the larger wigwams, and on opposite sides of the fire mats were spread. Then Smith, with his hands firmly bound, was brought in by his guards, and after being seated upon a mat was left, for a short time, entirely alone. Presently a man, painted black, holding a gourd rattle in his hand, and covered above his head and shoulders with snakes and weasel's skins, bounded into the apartment, chanting an invocation; with a loud voice and many passionate gestures, he encircled the fire with a broad ring of Indian meal. When this was accomplished, three others came rushing in, painted particoloured, in black, red, and white. After dancing and gesticulating for a while, these last were joined by three more, painted red about the eyes, and with their blackened faces relieved by streaks of white. These also danced about their prisoner in a savage and grotesque manner, and then they all sat down opposite to Smith, three on the one side of the chief medicine-man, and three on the other.

They now commenced a song. When it was ended, the chief medicine-man laid down five grains of corn. After working himself into such a passionate phrensy that his veins swelled out like cords, and the perspiration was visible in large drops, he began a short oration, at the conclusion of which they all gave a groan. Many other brief orations followed, all of which were terminated by a groan, and the dropping of three additional grains, until the fire was twice encircled by these little heaps of corn. Small bundles of sticks were now laid with similar ceremonies between each division of corn. When the approach of night put an end to the conjurations, which had been performed fasting, they all ate and drank heartily, and then retired. The conclusion to which the priests arrived, after three days spent in this manner, may be reasonably inferred from what followed.

All this time, Powhattan the emperor, standing apparently upon his dignity, waited at Werowocomoco until the captive should be brought before him. When Smith reached there, the procession was increased at the entrance of the town by the addition of two hundred warriors. It now halted, till Powhattan, arrayed in his robes of dignity, gave permission for the captive to be admitted into his presence.

In his royal dwelling, upon a raised seat, sat King Powhattan, covered with a great robe made of raccoon-skins. On each side of him sat a young girl of sixteen or eighteen years; and, stretching along both walls of the house were two rows of men, and behind them, as many women. Standing near the feet of Powhattan, was an Indian maiden, some thirteen years of age, clad in a succinct robe of the pliantest deer-skin, prettily fringed, and musical with tinkling ornaments. Around her neck she wore several long necklaces of white beads, through which her left arm was looped, after the custom of the Indian girls in those days. It was Pocahontas, the favourite daughter of King Powhattan.

When the captain entered, all the people gave a great shout; but Pocahontas, flinging back the jet black hair from her swarthy brow, gazed eagerly upon the bearded face of the wonderful white warrior, and uttered never a word.

Food was now brought and set before Smith.

The queen of Appomattox attended him with water to wash his hands, while another stood by to hand him a bunch of feathers, instead of a towel, to dry them.

After he had eaten, a long consultation was held by Powhattan and his swarthy advisers in relation to the future disposal of their prisoner. The conclusion they came to had at least the merit of being summary.

Two great stones were brought in and placed upon the ground before Powhattan. At a signal from the latter, as many warriors as could grasp the prisoner sprang toward him, and dragged him, struggling fiercely, to where the stones were set. Upon these, some forced their captive to lay his head, while others stood behind, with their war-clubs upraised, ready to beat out his brains.

During this scene of excitement and terror, the Princess Pocahontas stood near by, agitated beyond measure at the impending fate of the brave young soldier. Seeing the warriors nerving themselves to strike, she broke away from those who would have restrained her, and seizing the head of Smith in her arms, laid her own head upon his, saving, by this heroic act, the life of England's worthiest adventurer, and making her name immortal in the annals of the new world. Two days after this unexpected deliverance, Powhattan released Smith from his imprisonment, and sent him under the conduct of twelve guides to Jamestown.

Before the emperor took leave of his captive, he made him promise to bestow upon the guides two great guns and a grindstone, for the use of their master.

In two days they reached the fort, and after the savages were refreshed, Smith, mindful of his promise, pointed out to the servant of Powhattan two small pieces of cannon and a mill-stone, and bade him instruct his companions to carry them to Werowocomoco; but, says the old chronicler with a grim smile, when they essayed to lift them they found them somewhat too heavy, and were fain to put up with toys and such like gewgaws instead.

Most fortunate was it for the safety of the colony that Smith was returned there so unexpectedly. Only forty men remained alive, while the malcontents, consisting of those who called themselves the better sort, were making their preparations once more to run away with the pinnace, intending to leave their preacher, Mr. Hunt, and twenty-seven others, to their fate. For the third time, at the hazard of his life, Smith forced the conspirators to abandon their enterprise.

Finding their plans thus foiled, the wretched and malignant men, with Ratcliffe the governor at their head, turned upon Smith himself, and plotted to put him to death by the Levitical law for the loss of the two men who had been slain by the savages. They little knew with whom they had to deal. Before they could consummate their plans, they found themselves under arrest by the orders of Smith, who did not hesitate to imprison the principals until he could send them back to England.

CHAPTER V.

Arrival of the second supply—Newport opens a trade with Powhattan—Is outwitted by the emperor—Sagacity of Smith—Value of blue beads—Mania for gold-seeking in Virginia—Arrival of the Phœnix—Smith explores the Chesapeake—Returns to Jamestown—Sails, and completes his discoveries—Character of Smith—Elected governor of Virginia—Arrival of the third supply—Coronation of Powhattan—His regal intractability—Affairs at Jamestown—Energetic conduct of Smith—Powhattan attemps to starve out the colony—Expedition of Smith to Werowocomoco.

The return of Newport from England with fresh though limited supplies, and one hundred and twenty immigrants, had the effect of abating for a little while the distracted condition of the colony. This happening shortly after the release of Smith, word was quickly sent to Powhattan that Newport had come back to Jamestown, and was preparing to pay him a visit. To make his reception gracious in advance, Newport sent Powhattan many presents, which he had brought over for him, and with the latter expressed himself much pleased.

Taking with him in the pinnace a quantity of

goods adapted, as he supposed, to the peculiar tastes of the Indians, Newport, accompanied by Smith, set sail, and in due time reached Werowocomoco, where they were received by Powhattan in his usual barbarous state.

After having been duly feasted, and the customary songs and dances were over, Newport proposed to Powhattan to barter such commodities as he had brought with him for corn, of which the colony stood in great need.

Vulgar trade, however, the wily emperor affected to despise. "Captain Newport," said he, "it is not agreeable to my greatness, to truck in this peddling manner for trifles. I am a great Werowance; and I esteem you as the same; therefore, lay me down all your commodities together: what I like I will take, and in return you shall have what I conceive to be their value."

Smith reminded Captain Newport of the hazard he would incur by accepting the proposition; but Newport, being a vain man, and expecting to dazzle Powhattan by his bounty, complied with his request, and it unluckily proved as Smith had predicted. "The corn," said the latter, "might as well have been purchased in old Spain; we received but four bushels, when we expected twenty hogsheads."

Smith next tried his hand, and relied for success, not upon the emperor's sagacity, but on his simplicity. He accordingly took some toys, or gewgaws, and by glancing them dexterously in the light, they showed to great advantage.

Powhattan soon fixed his observing eye upon a string of blue beads, and became anxious to obtain them. Smith, however, seemed only the more unwilling to part with them; "they being," as he said, "composed of a most rare substance of the colour of the skies, and fit only to be worn by the greatest kings in the world." But the more reluctant Smith affected to be, the more eager Powhattan grew to become the owner of such precious jewels; and a bargain was at length struck between the subtle captain and the emperor, to the entire satisfaction of both parties; by which Smith obtained, for a pound or two of blue beads, two or three hundred bushels of corn.

By the same coy method of traffic, he subsequently obtained at an equally small cost another large supply of corn from his old enemy, Opechancanough, King of Pamunkey.

Blue beads, being thus elevated into imperial symbols of enormous value, afterward grew in such estimation among the Indians, that none but great Werowances, and their wives and daughters, were permitted to wear them.

Newport, having brought over with him, besides the usual complement of poor gentlemen, sundry goldsmiths and refiners, the mania for searching out mines of the precious metals spread throughout all classes of the colonists. Smith, with his strong common sense, endeavoured to turn their thoughts into a more practical channel; but in vain. The refiners, with their golden promises, made all men their slaves. There was no talk now—no hope—no work; but dig gold—wash gold—refine gold—load gold, such a continual outcry about gold, that one mad fellow desired to be buried in the sands, lest they should by their art make gold of his bones.

And thus the weeks flew by, and the ships stayed, until the provisions which should have supported the colonists were eaten up in a vain search after that, which to the last was never found.

Smith never countenanced these golden schemes, but often told Captain Martin, that unless the refiners could show him substantial proofs, he was not enamoured with their dirty skill. Nothing tormented him more than to see all necessary business thus neglected. He advised Newport to freight the ship with cedar, which could be done at once, rather than linger out his time, to the great detriment of the colony and the heavy cost of his employers. Newport, however, who, though a good seaman, was a self-opinionated man, preferred to load his ship with spangled earth, and so he waited until the approach of spring, when he departed with his valueless burden.

He had not been long gone, when the Phœnix, commanded by Captain Nelson, arrived at Jamestown, to the great joy of the colonists, who had given her up as lost.

The captain of the Phœnix, being a less visionary man than his predecessor, agreed to freight his ship with cedar, and this being speedily accomplished, he set sail for England.

As soon as the colonists were left once more to follow their appropriate labours, Smith fitted out an open barge of three tons burden, and quitted Jamestown, with a crew of fourteen men, to explore the waters of the Chesapeake Bay.

When he first set sail, some of his men, who were newly arrived in Virginia, and had yet to learn the indomitable character of their leader, loudly expressed their fears that on the first alarm he would return to the settlement, leaving the object of his expedition unaccomplished; but when they had been crowded in the small barge about two weeks, often tired at the oars, and with their bread so spoiled with wet that it had become partly rotten, they began to murmur at his obstinacy in still holding his resolution to proceed.

After enduring for some time their continual complaints and importunities, Smith addressed them in the following memorable words:

"Gentlemen, if you would remember the well-known history of Sir Ralph Lane, and how his company entreated him to proceed in the discovery of Moratico, alleging they had yet a dog remaining, which, being boiled with sassafras leaves, would richly feed them during their return; then what a shame it would be for you, who have been so suspicious of my timidity, to force me to put back, having so much provision, while scarcely able, as yet, to give any account of where we have been, and utterly ignorant of that which we were sent to seek.

"You cannot say I have not shared with you in the worst which is past; and for what is to come, either of lodging, diet, or whatsoever, I am contented to receive the worst part myself. As for your fears that I will lose myself in these large unknown waters, or be swallowed up in some stormy gust—abandon these childish fancies. Worse than has already been experienced is not likely to happen; and there is already as much danger in returning as in going forward. Regain therefore your old spirits, for return I will not—if it please God—till I have seen the Massawomacs, found the Potomac, or penetrated to the head of this water which you imagine to be endless."

After this decided expression of his will, all hope of changing his determination vanished. He did proceed. He did discover the Potomac. He sailed up that noble river, and crossing the country by land, examined a mine, the earth of which, so Newport had assured them, had been assayed in England and pronounced to contain large quantities of silver.

For seven weeks Smith continued his explorations, examining and noting every creek, harbour, and inlet, both on the eastern and western shores of the Chesapeake Bay. Many skirmishes and some sharp encounters he had with the natives; but by his coolness, sagacity, and skill, not one of his little company received any serious injury. The exhaustion of his provisions, and his own painful condition—he having been poisoned by a sea-nettle—compelled him at length to relinquish the further prosecution of his voyage, and return to Jamestown.

Such however was his energy, that three days had scarcely elapsed, before his barge, refitted and manned with twelve of the same crew, was once more floating down the James River, for the purpose of completing the previous discoveries.

This second exploration of the Chesapeake Bay ended with the most perfect results. Smith not only penetrated to the head of the bay, but also ascended its various tributaries as far as they were navigable. He held conferences with the Massawomacs, the Susquehannas, the Patuxents, and the Rappahannocks, fought with such as were hostile, and was friendly with all who met him in the same spirit; navigated the waters for forty-four days, sailed in that time some three thousand miles, and made a chart of the whole region, with its rivers, creeks, islands, harbours, and inlets, which has been valued for its correctness down to the present time.

And here, perhaps, is the most fitting place to exhibit one other bright phase in the character of this remarkable man.

Bred from his youth a soldier, he was yet singularly free from those vices which so frequently attach themselves to such as follow the profession of arms. He neither drank wine, swore oaths, nor gambled; but it was his daily custom to preface the duties of the morning by prayer and the singing of a psalm. This pious habit the keen-eyed savages soon remarked, and whenever afterward in their discourses to the whites they had occasion to speak of the Deity, they invariably referred to him as "the God of Captain Smith."

In regard to the conduct of Smith toward the natives, the opinions of men will naturally differ; but he who seeks to form a correct judgment in this matter, must weigh the acts of the young soldier by the standard of the times in which he lived, and not by the finer balance of the present day.

In all nobility of spirit; in self-abnegation where the wants of others conflicted with his own; in manly piety, energy, and daring; in soundness of judgment, quickness of decision in emergencies, and in the art of winning the love of all with whom he came in contact,—except, perhaps, the most depraved,—he will compare worthily with the most popular of those who have been called heroes, either in ancient or in modern times.

On the 3d of September, 1608, Smith was elected governor of the colony. Newport arrived shortly after with seventy immigrants, among whom were Mistress Forest and Annie Burras, these being the first English women that settled in the colony. The council was reorganized by the admission of new members; and then, as Newport had brought with him a tinsel crown, a scarlet cloak, and other mock insignia of royalty, Smith was despatched to Powhattan for the purpose of bringing the latter to Jamestown, where Newport proposed to perform the ceremony of investiture and coronation.

But though Powhattan was always gratified at receiving presents from the English, he was by no means inclined to place the safety of his royal person in their hands. He therefore answered haughtily.

"If your king has sent me presents, I also am a king, and this is my land; eight days I will remain here to receive them. Newport is to come to me, not I to him, nor to your fort. I will not bite at such a bait."

Accordingly, Newport, finding the emperor intractable, was compelled to go in person to Werowocomoco.

The next day was appointed for the coronation. As soon as the time arrived, the presents were brought in. They consisted of a ewer and bason, a bedstead with its customary furniture, a gay scarlet cloak, and other apparel, and a gilded crown.

After much ado and solicitation, King Powhattan suffered himself, though with great reluctance, to be inducted into his regal habiliments; but neither persuasion nor argument could induce him to kneel for the purpose of receiving his crown. Though the English self-constituted masters of ceremonies sought to explain that such was the approved and fashionable method in use among his brother monarchs in the old world, kneel he would not.

The difficulty, however, was at length happily removed, by some of them leaning heavily on the emperor's shoulder, which causing him to stoop a little, three of the company, lifting the crown between them, placed it upon his head.

And thus ended the coronation of King Powhattan, who did not forget that it was the duty of a monarch to bestow largesse upon any occasion which implied increase of dignity; in token whereof, he graciously presented Newport with his cast-off mantle and old shoes!

The state of affairs at Jamestown, under the rigid supervision of Governor Smith, quickly assumed a more promising aspect.

Buildings were erected and renovated; the

church repaired; the fort altered and strengthened; a military guard organized, and trained in squads daily; while every Saturday, the whole of the colonists were exercised in arms on the plain by the west bulwark.

The savages too, well knowing the character of the man with whom they would now have to deal, became all at once remarkably friendly and conciliating. The Princess Pocahontas also visited the town occasionally, with her wild followers, always bringing with her presents of corn, and game, and fruit, as substantial evidences of her regard.

In assigning the various duties in the way of labour among the colonists, Smith spared none. The rustic, in his eyes, was equal to the gentleman; or, rather, he regarded the former as a more important member of the body politic, especially if he was able-bodied and an efficient master of his craft. Nor did the brave young governor spare himself. Whatever was to be done, he led the way, and bade others profit by the example.

Thirty of them he took down the river some five miles below Jamestown, where he taught them to cut down trees and make clap boards; but the axes so often blistered the delicate fingers of the labouring gentlemen, that almost every third stroke was accompanied by an oath.

Smith's remedy for idleness was no food, and

a very excellent remedy it proved. His recipe for the cure of profane swearing was far more whimsical, but equally successful. He had a regular account kept of the number of expletives which each man gave vent to; and at night, for every separate oath, a can of cold water was poured down the sleeve of the offender.

A few rigid applications of the prescribed penalty effected so complete a cure of the propensity to swear, that in a little while scarcely an oath was to be heard in a week.

The continued influx of immigrants, notwithstanding the presents he had received, began to make Powhattan uneasy; and knowing that the colonists had never yet been able to raise more corn than was sufficient to subsist them for a few weeks, he directed his people to withhold their usual supplies of that necessary article of food.

This course of procedure, being persisted in, brought the condition of the colony down to the starving point. After several voyages in search of provisions had been made without success by his subordinates, Governor Smith, whom no persuasions could induce to starve quietly, determined to try whether he could not effect a better result by a journey to head-quarters, and an expedition was immediately organized for that purpose.

CHAPTER VI.

Smith sets out for Werowocomoco—Is visited by Powhattan—Smith's speech—Reply of Powhattan—Difficulties in the way of bartering for corn—Subtle conduct of the emperor—Smith and his companions surrounded by armed Indians—Rout of the latter—Supplies of corn obtained—Powhattan's treachery—Visit of Pocahontas—The project frustrated—Smith sails for Pamunkey—Is entertained by Opechancanough—Demands a supply of corn—Fearful situation of the whites—Smith takes Opechancanough prisoner—Surrender of his warriors—Their sudden friendship—The barges freighted with corn—Return to Jamestown.

On the 29th of December, 1608, Governor Smith out on his voyage to Werowocomoco. His acknowledged purpose was, either to trade with Powhattan for corn in a fair and impartial manner; or, if that was found impossible, to beat up the Indian head-quarters, and seize a supply of provision by force.

The expedition consisted of the pinnace of twenty tons, and the little barge used in the exploration of the Chesapeake Bay. The number of volunteers amounted to forty-six men.

On the 12th of January, after having been warned by the friendly chief of Warraskoyack that the intentions of Powhattan were of the most sanguinary nature, Smith reached the vicinity of Werowocomoco; but could not bring his vessels closer than within half a mile of the land, on account of the ice, which stretched far out into the Pamunkey river, and of the oozy marshes beyond.

This, however, did not deter the governor long. Breaking the thin edge of the ice so as to lay his vessels as near to the town as possible, he sprang from the bow of the barge, crossed the frozen space, and plunging into the mud and ooze, middle deep, called upon his companions to follow. As soon as all were landed, Smith took possession of the nearest houses, and sent a messenger to Powhattan, demanding refreshments for his men. Smothering his resentment, the emperor immediately complied with a request the peremptory character of which admitted of no evasion.

The next day he visited Smith in person. After stating that he had no corn for sale, and that he had not invited them there, he asked, with a gleam of his old spirit, how long the intruders intended to stay?

It happened, however, that Powhattan really had promised to freight the pinnace with corn, provided the governor would send him men to build a house, together with a specified number of guns and swords; a grindstone, and some copper and beads.

The men and the minor articles were despatched accordingly, but the weapons were prudently refused.

So when Powhattan protested he had neither sent for mechanics or merchandise; Smith, pointing to the men themselves, who were standing near by, asked the emperor how it was possible he could be so forgetful?

Finding himself thus palpably convicted of an untruth, Powhattan burst into a hearty laugh, and asked to be shown their commodities.

These were quickly displayed; but he would barter for nothing but guns and swords. Copper was freely offered him, but he would have nothing to do with it; telling them he could put a value upon his corn, but not upon their copper.

Smith, perceiving the intention of the emperor was not to trade at all, unless he could do it in his own way, threw aside aside all diplomacy, and addressed Powhattan in his usual plain, straightforward manner. "Powhattan," said he, "although I had many ways whereby I could have obtained the provisions I required, yet, believing in your promise to supply my wants, I neglected them all to satisfy your desire. To give you an evidence of my affection, I sent you my men to complete you a house, leaving my own unfinished. The corn your people had you have seized, forbidding them to trade with us; and now you think by consuming the time to make us perish with want, because we cannot comply with your strange demands. As for swords and guns, I told you long ago I had none to spare; and you well know that those I have can keep me from wanting food. Yet, steal from you, or wrong you, I will not; nor will I dissolve that friendship which has hitherto existed between us, unless you force me to do so by bad usage."

Having listened very attentively to this discourse, Powhattan promised that both he and his subjects would bring into the town whatever corn they had to spare within two days; and then turning with his grave, subtle manner toward the sturdy governor, he said:

"Captain Smith, it is the doubt I yet have of your true reasons for coming hither, that makes me refrain from relieving your wants. I have been informed by many persons that your object in coming here, is not to trade, but to possess my country and harass my people, who, seeing you and your men thus armed, are afraid to bring you their corn. To free us from this fear, leave your weapons aboard, for we being all friends they are needless here."

To this, however, Smith would by no means consent, and the day passed without either party yielding to the other.

The next morning, before the savages arrived with their supplies from the inland towns, Smith managed to obtain ten quarters of corn from Powhattan, in exchange for a copper kettle. With this barter both were well contented; but the emperor by no means relished trading with men who carried their weapons in one hand, and their commodities in the other. He began, therefore, another long discourse, eulogizing the blessings of peace, and expressing his wish to maintain friendly relations with his white neighbours. He said pathetically, that he had seen the death of three generations of his people, not one of whom was then living but himself; that he was very old, and must soon die, and that he desired to leave the whites on good terms with his successors.

Smith in reply, reminded Powhattan how often the savages had violated the promises which had been made in their behalf, and how kindly they had been treated notwithstanding. As for the wearing of arms, he said, that should not be construed into evil intentions, because they had repeatedly shown that it was not their wish to use them, except in self-defence, or to punish some aggressive act.

The old emperor, finding it almost impossible to make any impression upon the wary and uncompromising soldier, breathed a deep sigh, and said, in a tone of well-feigned reproach:

"Captain Smith, I never in my life used any chief so kindly as I have you; and yet, from you I have met with the least friendly return. Captain Newport gave me freely of every thing I desired, and received in return whatever I was pleased to offer. He would send away his guns at my request, and if you are disposed to show an equal friendship, let the men put aside their weapons, and I will believe you."

Smith, having at this time but eighteen men on shore, perceiving that Powhattan was only trifling with him until the hordes of armed savages, now flocking in from all quarters, should be able to surround his little band, quietly requested that some of the savages might be allowed to break the ice, so that his boat could approach the shore, and promised on the morrow he would land his followers unarmed.

To dissemble matters as long as possible, Powhattan gave permission to some of his people to open a passage for the boat, and while this was doing, having been informed that his warriors were ready to act, he left two or three of his women to engage Smith in conversation, while he secretly left the house in which the conference had been held. It was immediately surrounded by swarms of savages, but Smith was not the man to take these matters quietly. Without pausing until they should gain confidence from his indecision, he burst out at the doorway, and after discharging his pistol into the crowd, began to lay about him with his sword. Being well supported by his followers, the savages fled in the utmost confusion, falling one upon another in their eager efforts to escape.

A short time afterward, Powhattan sent a messenger to excuse his flight, on the plea that the approach of the boat filled with armed men had alarmed him, and that the multitude of his people, by whom the house was beset, had been sent by him, not with hostile intentions, but for the purpose of defending the corn from being taken away without his having received any equivalent remuneration for it.

A large quantity of corn had indeed been deposited near the house in baskets, and this fact gave some colour to the explanation which had been proffered. Smith received the excuse with a grim smile, but when the savages officiously proposed to take charge of the arms of his people while they carried the corn to the boat, he reversed the proposition by suggesting that they should throw down their bows and arrows, and load the boat with corn for him. As the suggestion of Smith, though quietly made, was doubtless accompanied by a significant show of weapons on the part of his men, the savages thought it best to acquiesce in the new arrangement. Stimulated by their fears, the corn was soon taken on board, and Smith would have quitted the place at once, but the ebb having left his barges firmly imbedded in the ooze, he was compelled to remain where he was until the next high tide should float them.

In the mean time, the savages seemed to have forgotten their fears and their enmity. They entertained the strangers with all manner of joyous sports and games, until it grew dark, when they all returned to Powhattan, who was in the woods at some distance, busily engaged in reorganizing his forces to surprise Smith in the night.

It is impossible to say what might have been the issue of this scheme, if Smith had remained entirely ignorant of the design; but, fortunately, his former gentle preserver, the youthful Princess Pocahontas, threaded secretly the dark woods and put him upon his guard.

She told Smith, that under pretence of providing himself and his companions with a bountiful supply of refreshments for their evening meal, a number of men would be introduced, whose instructions were to seize the weapons of his men while they were at supper, and then murder them. If this stratagem was unsuccessful, then an attempt was to be made by a large body of men approaching unawares from without. She entreated him therefore to quit the place at once; but this Smith would not do, neither would he take refuge on board of his boats. Thanking Pocahontas most warmly and gratefully for the warning she had given him, he pressed upon her a number of trinkets, such as she usually delighted in; but she would accept of none, lest their being found upon her person should lead her father to suspect she had betrayed his plans; a suspicion which, if confirmed in any way, might involve the safety of her own life. So with many tears she tore herself from them, and departed alone through the dark woods as secretly as she came.

Within less than an hour after she had left, eight or ten stout savages came to the house, bearing huge platters of cooked venison and other food. Affecting to be almost suffocated with the smoke of the matches, which were used in those days for the purpose of firing off the guns, they importuned Smith to have them quenched. This modest request was of course refused by the soldier, who, suspecting that possibly the food which they had brought might have been tampered with, compelled each of the savages to partake of a portion of it, before he permitted his men to satisfy their appetites. When they had done so, he sent several of them back to Powhattan, to inform him that his intentions were known, and that he might come on as soon as he pleased, as they were fully prepared to receive him.

This bold invitation quite frustrated the project of the emperor, and although a strict watch was kept up the whole of the night, the morning dawned at length without their having received any molestation.

At high-water the next day the barges floated, and when all his followers were once more safely on board, Smith exchanged courtesies with the savages who thronged the banks to see them off, and dropped down the river to Pamunkey. When they reached the vicinity of the latter town, they were entertained by Opechancanough, with a great show of regard. After remaining there three days, Smith, taking with him a detachment of fourteen men, proceeded to the town, a quarter of a mile from the river, which they found deserted by all its usual inhabitants, except a lame man and a boy.

It was not long, however, before Opechancanough arrived, accompanied by a considerable number of armed men, but with scarcely any of the provisions he had promised.

Finding himself likely to receive but a scanty supply, unless he took decided steps to procure it, Smith turned to Opechancanough, and after reminding him that the previous year he had freighted with corn the ship which had been sent to him, said with his usual bluntness:

"You know my want, and as I am equally conscious of your plenty, I am resolved by some means to have a portion of it. Here are my commodities; take your own choice first, and after you have selected such as you prefer, I will barter the remainder with your people."

Upon these terms an exchange was immediately made, the king promising the next day to bring down a further and a larger supply. Accordingly, when the time came, Smith again proceeded to the town, where he at first found only four or five men, each newly arrived, with a great basket of corn. Opechancanough made his appearance with some forty or fifty of his followers soon after, and held Smith in conversation until some seven hundred warriors, completely armed, had surrounded the house.

Some of Smith's companions expressing a fear of their inability to withstand such numbers, the captain made light of the danger, and told them, at the worst, they could fight like men, and not die like sheep, for "by that means," said he, "God hath often delivered me before, and so I trust will now."

When the king saw that his designs were suspected, he sought to restore confidence by ordering a large present of corn to be brought and laid outside the door. This, however, was but a stratagem to draw Smith and his companions from the house; for lying behind a great tree that was blown down, were numbers of warriors, with their bows bent ready to shoot, the moment any of the whites attempted to pass the door.

Indignant at being encompassed about in this manner, Smith took his resolve at once. He sprang into the midst of the warriors within the house, and seizing Opechancanough by his scalp-lock, planted a pistol against his breast, and led him a prisoner to the door, so that the danger in which their king was could be seen by all his people.

This energetic act disarmed the warriors at once. Seeing their king a prisoner, they threw aside their weapons, brought in corn in abundance, and strove to atone by a show of eager friendship for their previous hostility. No further interruption occurred; the corn was taken to the barges, as at Werowocomoco, on the backs of the people, and when the loading was completed, Smith set sail for Jamestown.

CHAPTER VII.

Return of Smith to Jamestown—Loss of Scrivener, Gosnoll, and others—Government of Smith—Activity of the colonists—Growing scarcity of food—Many settlers quartered around Jamestown—Insubordination—Firmness of Smith—Arrival of Captain Argall—The commissioners in England surrender their charter—A new commission granted—Lord de la Warre appointed Governor-general of Virginia—Nine vessels sail from England for the colony—Parted in a storm—Uncertain fate of the flag ship—The others of the fleet arrive in Virginia—Difficulties with Smith—His resolute conduct—Opens several new plantations—Powhattan settled—Terrible accident to Smith—His return to England—Statistics of the colony—Its prosperous condition.

THE return of Smith to Jamestown was hastened by the tidings of an unhappy accident which had occurred during his absence. This was no other than the loss of Mr. Scrivener, Captain Waldo, Anthony Gosnoll, and eight others, by the upsetting of their boat in a storm on the James River.

He had no sooner reassumed the reins of government than the colony began to feel the beneficial effects of his watchfulness and energy.

Having succeeded in obtaining during his late voyage nearly five hundred bushels of corn, and two hundred pounds of deer suet, he considered an economical disposition of this supply sufficient to last the colonists for three months, or until their own harvest came round.

His anxieties in regard to provision being thus put to rest, he now determined to maintain no idlers, but that all should labour equally for the common benefit. The whole of the colonists were therefore divided into companies of ten and fifteen each, separate duties allotted to each company, and the period of labour, six hours of each day, strictly enforced. The firmness with which an exact performance of these rules was insisted upon soon roused the old spirit of insubordination among the gentlemen colonists, who imagined their birth and condition ought to exempt them from the degradation of working for a subsistence.

But Governor Smith would admit of no exceptions. He did not even shield himself, under cover of his office, from the performance of those tasks which he required of others. He demanded no more than that all the ablest bodied colonists should equal him in industry.

When therefore he perceived a mutinous spirit among those who esteemed themselves as the better class, and that they were disposed to disobey the rules he had laid down, he took a short but most effectual method of reducing them to obedience. Having entire control of the public stores, from which each colonist received his rations daily, Smith decreed that those who did not work should not eat; and hunger being a forcible stimulant to industry, after a few of the malcontents had tested to their satisfaction the operation of the law, they found it far pleasanter to submit than to resist.

During the three months thus busily employed, the colonists got ready for the ships, whose arrival was expected, large quantities of pitch, tar, pot-ashes; and succeeded in manufacturing a small supply of glass, most probably for their own use. They also constructed nets and wears for fishing; built some twenty houses; thatched the church with reeds from the adjoining marsh; sank a well in the fort; and built a block-house on the point of the peninsula, for the purpose of overawing the savages. In addition to these labours, thirty acres of land were broken up and planted with corn, and two other block-houses, easy of defence, erected in commanding situations.

Owing to the vast increase of rats in the colony, the corn, which had been stored away in casks, was found upon examination to have been so seriously depredated upon, that the supply was exhausted much earlier than was expected, and as the season for gathering their own corn had not yet arrived, several detachments of the colonists were sent from Jamestown, and quartered in other places, for the better convenience of obtaining food.

Under any other governor than Smith, this policy might have been considered injudicious, as it weakened his effective force, and exposed his parties to be beaten in detail by the savages. But so great was the terror with which he had inspired the Indians, so prompt was he to repress the least show of hostilities, and so sleeplessly indefatigable was he in all he undertook, that the savages well knowing a bloody retaliation would follow any overt act on their part, were constrained to continue peaceful even when the colonists were most open to their attacks.

But while he thus held the savages in check by the mere terror of his name, Smith had a far more difficult task in preserving subordination among his own people. While food was plentiful he succeeded in repressing disorders; but no sooner did the supplies begin to fail, than idlers and malcontents became so abundant, that he was compelled to resort to severer measures than any he had yet ventured upon. A large number of the colonists, after importuning him unsuccessfully to barter every article they possessed, even their weapons, for a few baskets of corn yet remaining among the Indians, had determined among themselves to force him to comply with their wishes, by refusing to do any thing toward providing for their own daily wants.

Smith was the last man in the world whom they could have hoped to drive into any act to which his judgment was opposed, and they soon found him such.

He called a meeting of the people, and addressing himself particularly to the disaffected, he pointed out what he had already done for the good of the colony, and how it had more than once been preserved through his exertions. Referring to their refusal to hunt, or fish, or even to gather wild fruits, he said:

"I will take such measures as shall compel you to provide for yourselves of such food as is to be obtained. The sick shall be exempt from service, and shall share equally with us all; but he who, being well, does not bring in as much provision every day as I do, shall be banished from the fort on the morrow, and set beyond the river, until such time as he is willing to fulfil this regulation, or starve."

This order many considered as unnecessarily harsh, but the obedience it demanded was rendered nevertheless; and so, amid plottings and murmurings, the affairs of the colony moved jarringly on until the arrival of Captain Argall, with a ship well furnished with wine and provision.

The letters brought by Argall contained much censure of Smith, for the decided manner in which he had dealt with the savages, and communicated at the same time the startling intelligence of the surrender of the Virginia patent into the hands of King James, and the issue of a new commission, under which Lord Delaware was appointed governor-general of Virginia; Sir Thomas Gates, his lieutenant; Sir Thomas Dale, high-marshal; Sir Ferdinand Wainman, general of the horse; Captain Newport, vice-admiral, together with various other officers, sufficient in number to have governed an established kingdom, rather than the few miserable, half-starved colonists, who had only been kept together by the incessant care of Captain Smith.

One good effect, however, was promised by the surrender of the old charter. Under the new organization, the commissioners speedily raised such large sums of money as enabled them to despatch nine ships and five hundred immigrants to Jamestown. The command of this fleet was given to Newport. Sir Thomas Gates and Sir George Somers accompanied the latter, armed with power to cancel the old commissions, and assume authority in the colony until the arrival of Lord Delaware.

These three officers sailed together from England, in May, 1609, in the flag-ship of the vice-admiral, the Sea-Venture; but being separated from the rest of the fleet in a severe storm, were for some time supposed to be lost. The other ships arrived in due season, and the immigrants they contained were disembarked. Among those who returned to the colony at this time, to the great indignation of Smith, were his old enemies Ratcliffe, Martin, and Archer.

A landing had no sooner been effected than the sturdy governor found his authority disputed. As the fate of the commissioners was uncertain, Smith resolved to retain his office until its term expired, unless previously superseded by the arrival of the commissioners, or by fresh orders from England. In carrying out this determination, he had occasion for the exercise of all that decision of character for which he was so remarkable. Surrounded by an unruly multitude, ignorant of his superior qualities, and instigated by all those who hated the salutary laws he had so rigidly enforced, he was subjected to a constant succession of conspiracies, by which his life was placed in continual danger.

Resolutely bent on maintaining his authority until it could be legally transferred into proper hands, Smith seized the chief conspirators, and imprisoned them in the fort. Those of less note he sent away from Jamestown to garrison some of the outposts, where their enmity could be tempered by a due regard for their personal safety. By this means, he succeeded in repressing that condition of unbridled license with which the colony was threatened, and in preserving a fair share of decorum and regularity.

No sooner, however, was his year of office expired, than he surrendered his authority to Captain Martin; but the latter was so conscious of his own inefficiency, that, after retaining the governorship for three hours, he resigned it again into the hands of Smith.

The large influx of colonists enabling Smith to open plantations at a distance from the city, he sent Captain West with one hundred and twenty men to build a fort near the falls of James River, and cultivate the land adjacent. Finding, on a subsequent personal inspection, that the situation upon which the fort had been erected was a disadvantageous one, in consequence of being subject to overflow from the river, the governor treated with the emperor for his ancient seat of Powhattan. This was a fine healthy location, the town being strongly fortified with pickets, the houses in good repair, with two hundred acres of cleared land adjoining.

When the conditions of sale were agreed upon, another and most unexpected difficulty arose. West's people, being mostly new-comers, and not inclined either to acknowledge the authority of Smith, or to submit to his advice, determined to remain at their new settlement. Though the governor had but five men with him, he attempted to force the refractory settlers to obey his wishes, but was beaten off. Capturing the boat containing all their provision, he attached it to his own barge, and stood off from the place, intending to starve them into submission. After nine days spent in a vain attempt to bring them to a sense of their duty, during which time the savages came daily with complaints of their disorderly conduct, Smith set sail.

He had scarcely departed, before the exasperated Indians, after attacking and killing some of the stragglers, assaulted the fort. Smith, whose vessel had at this time grounded upon a bar about a mile and a half below, immediately put back; but the Indians had already fled with their booty. The garrison, now thoroughly alarmed, submitted themselves unconditionally to the mercy of the governor. Taking with him, as prisoners, six or seven of the ringleaders, he conveyed the remainder to Powhattan, and after appeasing the Indians, and appointing new officers to command the garrison, was about to take his departure, when Captain West arrived. At the earnest intercession of the latter, Smith released his prisoners, and delivered up the ammunition and provision he had previously captured. No sooner was this done than the men grew as turbulent as before. Conscious of his inability to cope with such numbers, Smith left the place in disgust, and set out for Jamestown.

It was during this return voyage that the sad accident occurred which deprived Virginia of the future services of him who is most emphatically entitled to the honour of being styled the founder of the colony.

While sleeping in the boat, the powder-bag he constantly carried upon his person was accidentally set on fire by one of the crew. The explosion tore away some nine or ten inches of flesh from his body, and the burning of his garments occasioned such exquisite torment, that he leaped in his agony into the river, where he came near drowning before he was rescued. In this painful condition he reached Jamestown.

There being no surgeon in the colony, Smith made arrangements for the proper defence of the settlement during his absence, and after deputing his authority to Captain George Percy, took passage for England on board one of the ships then lying in the harbour.

When he was compelled, by reason of his painful wound, to cross the ocean for medical advice, the prosperity of the colony was daily increasing. It contained nearly five hundred inhabitants, had ten weeks' provision in the public store, was possessed of an abundance of arms and ammunition, implements of all kinds, and a supply of clothing amply sufficient for the wants of the settlers. The live stock of the colony at this period consisted of six brood mares and a horse, some six hundred swine, an equal number of fowls, and a few goats and sheep.

Jamestown, which contained some fifty or sixty houses, Smith had taken especial pains to fortify in the strongest manner, and had also caused to be opened, at various distances from the town, above and below, some five or six plantations, on each of which a strong block-house had been erected, for the protection of such as were engaged in agricultural pursuits in the vicinity.

When we consider the class of persons of which the colony of Virginia was mainly composed, it is still more astonishing that so much should have been effected. There were only one good and three indifferent carpenters among the whole of the immigrants; and but two blacksmiths. Those who came under the denomination of labourers were merely serving-men brought over by various adventurers to attend upon them personally, or such idle roisterers as had never before performed a day's work in their life. All the rest were poor gentlemen, decayed tradesmen, libertines, and the like, whom neither the fear of God, nor the law, nor shame, nor the displeasure of their friends, could rule at home. It was a sorrowful day for Virginia, when the disabled condition of the only man fitted by nature and education to control this mixed and unruly body of settlers, constrained him to take his departure from the shores of the new world.

CHAPTER VIII.

Captain George Percy—His reasons for remaining in the colony—His ill-health—Factious spirit of the people—Indian hostilities—Massacre of Ratcliffe and his men—West and thirty others turn pirates—Miserable condition of the colonists—Arrival of Sir Thomas Gates and Sir George Sommers—The colony deserted—Arrival of Lord Delaware—His judicious measures—The colony begins to flourish—Delaware returns to England—Disappointment of the London company—Sir Thomas Dale sent to Virginia — His arrival—Proclaims martial law—Sir Thomas Gates arrives at Jamestown—Assumes the government of the colony—A plantation opened at Henrico—Private property recognised in the colony—Beneficial results arising therefrom—New Bermudas settled—The third charter of the London company—Change in the constitution—Money allowed to be raised by lottery for the benefit of the colony.

When Captain George Percy, in 1609, consented, at the instance of Smith, to accept the office which the latter was compelled to resign, it was from an earnest desire to serve the colony to the best of his ability. He had previously intended to seek the restoration of his own failing health by a voyage to England; but well knowing that so soon as Smith had taken his departure, the comparatively small number of industrious and well-disposed settlers would fall a prey to those reckless and unprincipled adventurers who were already feared by their own countrymen, and hated by the savages, he concluded to remain and endeavour to preserve something like order, until the officers duly appointed should arrive from England.

Increasing ill-health, however, prevented him from exercising his authority effectively, and the condition of the colony soon became deplorable. The community was broken up into numerous factions; a dozen vile and worthless leaders claimed the supremacy, while their deluded followers were encouraged to live in the most shameless and abandoned manner.

The Indians who had shown themselves friendly were grossly maltreated. Profiting by the absence of Smith, they broke out into open war. They attacked and destroyed the plantations of Martin and West, and killed nearly one-half of their men; the remainder fled to Jamestown. Thirty men, sent out under Ratcliffe to trade with Powhattan, were all surprised and slain, with the exception of two, whose lives were preserved by the Princess Pocahontas. West, who with a like number had been appointed to a similar duty, deserted with his crew, and commenced a career of piracy. The supply of provisions was soon consumed. The hogs, goats, sheep, horses, were next devoured; and then every article that could be traded away to the Indians, even to the armour and weapons of defence, was exchanged for food. When these failed, they prolonged a miserable existence upon berries and roots. Day by day they died, either by the weapons of the savages or from sheer starvation. Within six months from the departure of Smith, only sixty men survived. Those remaining could not have supported life for ten days longer, when they were miraculously preserved from the fate of their companions.

On the 24th of May, 1610, Sir Thomas Gates and Sir George Sommers arrived from the Bermudas with one hundred and sixty men. Parted from the rest of the ships by a storm at sea, they had been driven, water-logged, upon those rocky islands, and from the wreck of their vessels had constructed two small barks to bear them to Virginia.

They expected to meet a prosperous colony, and found nothing but famine and a mere handful of gaunt and haggard men. Utterly dismayed at the prospect before them, they yielded to the general wish, and set sail for Newfoundland, hoping to obtain food for the company among the fishing vessels which frequented that coast.

On the 7th of June, they abandoned the scene of so much misery; and it was with difficulty the colonists could be persuaded from setting fire to the town. But it was not the will of Heaven that so fine a country should be suffered to return to its original wildness.

The next morning, when near the mouth of the river, they fell in with the longboat of Lord

Delaware, who had arrived on the coast with three ships well furnished with all needful supplies. With great difficulty the fugitives were prevailed upon to return, and the same night they again landed at Jamestown.

The following day, the 10th of June, 1610, while the impression of their unexpected deliverance rendered them yet profoundly grateful, the colonists, preceded by Lord Delaware and the officers who had accompanied him, entered the little church which Smith had newly thatched, and within the walls of that rude but sacred edifice, supplicated forgiveness for past errors, and in all humility compared their condition to that of the children of Israel, whom the arm of the Lord of hosts conducted through the Red Sea and the wilderness, before he suffered them to possess, in prosperous tranquillity, the fertile land of Canaan.

After the sermon was over, Lord Delaware instituted an inquiry into the causes of the late disasters. Finding them to have proceeded from the insubordination of the colonists themselves, he reproached them with firm seriousness for the evils they had wrought, and entreated them to amend past follies.

His commission having been read, he told them he was resolved to exercise his authority, mildly and paternally if possible; but that if he was compelled to proceed rigidly against the refractory, he should not hesitate to enforce submission with the sword.

Regulations were soon after proclaimed for the government of the colonists; officers were appointed, and each man allotted his particular duty. The effect of this was gratifying in the extreme. Six hours of each day were set apart for labour, the rest might be appropriated to pastime. Nor were the offices of religion forgotten. Before and after labour, all entered the little church, the approach to which was kept prettily adorned with native wild-flowers, and joined in brief devotional exercises, from which none were excused, unless unable to attend from sickness, or some other justifying cause.

Under the new administration no idlers were suffered. Even the gentlemen had duties assigned to them proportioned to their ability. The dwellings were repaired and improved; covered above with strong boards, and matted round with Indian mats. The forts were garrisoned, and savage hostilities successfully restrained. But while the colony under the judicious care of the new governor was daily increasing in prosperity, the health of Lord Delaware became so seriously impaired as to compel him to return to England. Sir Thomas Gates having previously left Virginia for the mother country, and Sir George Sommers being absent on a voyage to the Bermudas, the government was again intrusted to Captain

Percy. At the time Lord Delaware left the colony, it consisted of two hundred men, and was supplied with provisions for ten months. His unexpected arrival in England was a source of great mortification to the London Company, who had already debated for some time, and with great anxiety, the propriety of sustaining any longer a colony whose reverses had been so many, and the returns from which had been so meager.

The serious representation of Sir Thomas Gates, of the benefits which would ultimately accrue from a proper support of the colony, induced them to persevere in their endeavours to sustain it; and before Lord Delaware reached England, Sir Thomas Dale had been despatched to Virginia with three ships, freighted with immigrants and supplies.

He arrived safely at Jamestown on the 10th of May, 1611, and found the colonists fast relapsing into their old habits of improvidence. They had neglected even to plant corn, relying upon the public store for supplies. Though the season was already advanced, Dale, on assuming the government, at once directed that corn should be planted, and under his vigorous supervision a tolerable crop was secured.

As if conscious of the inefficiency with which the colony had been governed, the authority of Sir Thomas Dale had been enlarged by the London Company. Martial law was established;

crime was punished in a summary manner, and the duties of religion enforced by military rules.

Perhaps this severe and arbitrary system was, after all, the best calculated to maintain order in the colony. Indulgence and a weak yielding to the passions of the people had brought them more than once to the very brink of destruction; while under established rules, rigidly enforced, they had always managed to prosper.

Sir Thomas Dale, a worthy and experienced soldier in the Low Countries, while he resolutely repressed disorder, by no means exceeded the limits of his authority. His brief administration was attended with the happiest results. His letters to England, while confessing the smallness of the colony, expressed hopes which cheered the patrons of the enterprise, and induced them to follow up their late liberality by increased exertions. Sir Thomas Gates was despatched from London with six ships and three hundred men, and arrived at Jamestown on the 2d of August, 1611. This new supply was so unexpected, that at first the colonists mistook the vessels for a hostile fleet.

Gates now assumed the government, to the great joy of the colonists, who now numbered seven hundred men. Fully appreciating the difficulties overcome by his predecessor, he approved all his acts, and assented to a design which Dale had already formed.

This was no other than to open a large plantation higher up the river. To further the object, Sir Thomas Gates furnished his friend with three hundred and fifty men, or one-half of the whole number of colonists. They were a selected company. Late in September, Dale, having already chosen a site for his new settlement, protected it with palisades, and called the place Henrico, in honour of Prince Henry, the eldest son of James I.

The next work he did was to build at each corner of the town a high commanding blockhouse; then he erected a church and storehouses, and when these were finished, he constructed excellent dwellings for himself and his men.

This town was situated upon a neck of land, surrounded on three sides by the river, and on the fourth well palisadoed. It had three streets of well-framed houses, a handsome church, and the foundation of another, to be constructed in a more substantial manner of brick, besides storehouses, block-houses, and similar structures. Along the verge of the river, at stated distances, were five other strongly-built houses, from which a continual watch was kept for the security of the town.

One of the immediate benefits arising from the administration of Gates was the recognition of private property. Hitherto all had laboured alike for the common good, and were clothed and fed from the public store. Having no stimulus for exertion, and the idle or sluggish receiving the same allotment of apparel and provision as the laborious and the energetic, men grew disheartened at a distribution which neither recognised merit nor rewarded industry.

So discouraging was this state of things, that frequently, in the best times, the labour of thirty men did not accomplish more than was done, under a different system, by three. It was the great merit of Gates that he saw at once where the evil lay, and applied the appropriate remedy. A few acres of land were given to each man for his orchard and garden, to cultivate as he thought proper, and to apply the proceeds to his own use, after paying a small portion of his produce to the general store, as a provision against contingencies. The consequences of this wise liberality were in the highest degree satisfactory; and henceforth every encouragement was afforded to individual enterprise in the acquisition of wealth. The rights of the Indians, however, were less regarded. In December, 1611, Sir Thomas Dale captured the town of Appamattuck, and driving off the savages, took possession of their houses and corn. Finding the place commodiously situated, and within an easy distance of Henrico, he immediately appropriated his conquest to the uses of a new settlement, which he called New Bermudas.

Under the same imperious patent, he laid out and annexed many miles of champaign and woodland, dividing the lands into several hundreds or districts, and building a number of houses along the frontier for the better security of the newly-acquired territory.

While Virginia was thus gradually extending her habitable limits, and enjoying a period of peace and prosperity, a new charter was granted by James to the London Company, by which all the former privileges and immunities were confirmed, and the period of exemption from duties extended.

By the new charter a great change was made in the constitution of the company. The sole power of ordering the affairs of the company had hitherto resided in a council, named in the charter, but whose vacancies were supplied by the majority of the corporation. This power was now taken from the hands of the council, and given to the stockholders, by whom the inferior transactions of the company might be discussed at weekly meetings, reserving the more important questions of government, commerce, and territory, for the four great and general courts, at which all officers were to be elected, and all laws established. This great change affected only the corporation, the political rights of the colonists remaining unimproved.

Another and more doubtful privilege was also

given by the new charter: it was that of raising money by lotteries for the benefit of the colony. These lotteries, after being tolerated for a few years, were found productive of so many evils, that upon the complaint of the Commons they were suspended by an order of council. In the mean while they had produced to the company nearly thirty thousand pounds.

CHAPTER IX.

Administration of Sir Thomas Gates—Cautious forbearance of Powhattan—Treachery of Japazaws—Capture of Pocahontas—She is taken to Jamestown—A ransom demanded for her release—Powhattan sends back men and muskets—Sir Thomas Dale sent to enforce the remainder of the ransom—Reaches Werowocomoco—Is assaulted—Defeats the savages and burns the town—Parleys with the Indians—Returns to Jamestown—John Rolfe instructs Pocahontas in the Christian faith—She is baptized—Marriage of Pocahontas to Rolfe—Satisfaction of Powhattan—Its beneficial consequences—Dale treats with Powhattan for another daughter—His refusal—Rolfe and his wife sail for England—Pocahontas honourably received—Her death at Gravesend.

The administration of Sir Thomas Gates was eminently judicious. The condition of the colonists was greatly ameliorated and improved, a spirit of industry was fostered, and the savages effectually restrained.

Powhattan was cautious and forbearing, resigning himself to the increase of the colonists, as to an evil which it was now too late to remedy.

An event at length occurred which threatened at first to involve the country in a sanguinary war. Its romantic termination fortunately led to a firmer and more lasting peace.

In 1612, Captain Argall was sent to the Potomac to purchase corn: while he remained in that river, he learned from Japazaws, an old chief, and a tried friend to the English, that the Princess Pocahontas was secreted in the neighbourhood. Singular enough, the daughter of Powhattan had never entered Jamestown from the day Smith left it; but had resided for some time on the shores of the Potomac, in the family of Japazaws. A scheme was now entered upon by Japazaws to betray her to the English, and Argall, well knowing the value of the prize, bribed the treacherous chief to entice her on board his vessel. This was effected by a cunning stratagem. The wife of Japazaws pretended to be exceedingly anxious to see one of the big canoes of the white people, while the old chief expressed himself vehemently in opposition to her going alone. The wife redoubled her entreaties, and Japazaws, as if losing all patience, threatened to chastise her unless she ceased her importunities. This harsh conduct producing a flood of tears, Japazaws pretended to relent, and consented that his wife should have her curiosity satisfied, provided the Princess Pocahontas would agree to accompany her. Little suspecting the snare which had been laid for her, the kind-hearted maiden consented. The members of the little party were courteously received in the cabin by Argall, and feasted with the best he could provide; Japazaws treading occasionally on the captain's foot to remind him that he had fulfilled his compact. When the hour arrived for their departure, Argall told Pocahontas she must return with him to Jamestown; whereupon Japasaws and his wife, with loud cries and lamentations, bewailed the manner in which their young charge had been taken prisoner. Pocahontas, also, at first, fell to weeping; but grew composed when she learned that the object of her detention was to hasten a treaty of peace between the colonists and her father. A copper-kettle and a few beads pacified Japazaws and his companion, both of whom left the vessel rejoicing that Pocahontas still believed them to be among her best and most devoted friends.

Pocahontas was treated with the utmost kindness and attention at Jamestown, and soon became reconciled to her captivity. In the mean while, messengers were sent to Powhattan, demanding a ransom. The conditions insisted upon were, that the emperor should return all the prisoners he had captured, and all the swords, guns, and implements which had been stolen at different times by his people. Powhattan loved his daughter dearly, but he was desirous of retaining both his prisoners and his spoils. The prisoners were useful to him as mechanics, and the spoils gratified his pride.

Nature, however, at length prevailed. After a silence of three months, he sent back seven of his prisoners, and the same number of unserviceable muskets. He also sent word, that if his daughter was released, he would atone satisfactorily for all the injuries which had been done to the colony, and remain for ever after a firm friend.

The council at Jamestown quietly accepted the prisoners and old muskets as part payment; but kept possession of his daughter until the remainder of the arms and implements which had been stolen were returned.

Powhattan was indignant. Discovering that they were not likely to make terms with him by diplomacy, the council resolved to resort to arms. Accordingly Sir Thomas Dale, having with him the Princess Pocahontas, and further accompanied by one hundred and fifty men well armed and equipped, set sail for Werowocomoco. When Dale reached the town, he was hailed from the shore, and the reason of his presence demanded. His reply was, that he had come to receive the ransom for the Princess Pocahontas, or to take it by force. He immediately received a spirited answer. They told him, if he chose to fight he was welcome to do so, as they were perfectly prepared for him; but if he valued his own life, or the lives of his men, they would advise him to retire, or they would use him as they had done Captain Ratcliffe.

Dale said he would have a better answer, and the reply was a flight of arrows.

But savage spirit, though supported by numbers, was no match for armed and disciplined men. The forces of Powhattan were speedily routed, and the town set on fire.

The next day, Dale proceeded higher up the river. He was again hailed by the Indians, and asked why he had attacked them and destroyed their town? "Why did you shoot at us?" was his reply. They said it was done by some straggling savages, and without their consent; that they did not intend to provoke hostilities, desiring rather to be friends. Dale responded in an equally pacific strain, and then sending messengers to Powhattan, proceeded further up the river. Here, at one of the royal houses, he encountered four hundred men, who desired him and his company to come ashore; but at the same time demanded a truce until they could send to Powhattan to know his pleasure. It was granted until the next day at noon.

When this short armistice had been agreed upon, the two brothers of Pocahontas presented themselves and requested an interview with their sister. When they found she was well in health and in excellent spirits, they were exceedingly rejoiced, and promised to use their best endeavours to persuade her father to redeem her and to become the firm friend of the colonists. With this promise Dale was obliged to be content. Powhattan resolutely refused to see the messengers which had been sent to treat with him, and the period of corn-planting approaching, Dale returned with Pocahontas to Jamestown and disbanded his men.

But the friendship of the aged Emperor Powhattan, which could neither be purchased by gifts nor influenced by threats, was at length to be acquired in a simple and a far more honourable manner.

John Rolfe, a young gentleman whose family connections were highly respectable, conceived the design of instructing Pocahontas in the doctrines of the Christian faith. He found the princess both quick and docile; and the labour for the conversion of the unregenerated maiden daily became less a task of duty than of love. Nor was the princess herself insensible to the endearing kindness of her amiable and enthusiastic instructor. She soon acquired a partial knowledge of the English tongue, and as her perceptions became clearer, the pure morality of the Christian religion won her willingly to embrace its doctrines. In the little rudely-constructed church at Jamestown, before the font, which was hewn out of the trunk of a tree, hollowed into the shape of a canoe, the Princess Pocahontas openly renounced her country's idolatry, professed the faith of Jesus Christ, and was baptized.

In April, 1613, with the full approbation of her father, she was married to John Rolfe. Powhattan not only authorized Sir Thomas Dale to give the bride away, but sent her uncle Opachisco and two of her brothers to be present at the ceremony.

The marriage between the Princess Pocahontas —now called the Lady Rebecca—and John Rolfe, won, not only the friendship of Powhattan and the various tribes over whom he exercised control, but induced the Chickahominies also to send messengers with presents to Sir Thomas Dale, excusing all former injuries, and desiring to form a treaty of alliance with him as new Englishmen, who were henceforth willing to become the subjects and tributaries of King James.

With a view to strengthen, to a still greater degree, the bonds of amity between the colonists and their barbarian neighbours, Sir Thomas Dale made a proposition to Powhattan for another of his daughters.

Master Ralph Hamor, his messenger, left Bermudas in the morning, and reached the royal residence of Powhattan the next evening. The aged king received his visitor but coldly; but to Thomas Savage, the interpreter, whom he knew well, he said: "My child, I gave you leave to visit your friends, and this is the first time I have seen you these four years past." Turning to Hamor, he asked him for the chain of pearl which he had given to Sir Thomas Dale as a token to pass between them whenever an approved messenger should be sent. Hamor, having neglected to bring it with him, plausibly denied the necessity of it at all, since he did not come alone, having been attended in his journey by two of Powhattan's own people. The emperor expressed himself satisfied with the explanation, and after presenting the messenger a pipe of tobacco, continued the conversation by asking how his brother Sir Thomas Dale did, and his daughter and unknown son; and how they lived, loved, and liked? Hamor told him that Sir Thomas Dale was well, and his daughter, the Lady Rebecca Rolfe, so well contented, she would not live with him again. Powhattan laughed, and then asked Hamor the cause of his coming. The latter replied that the message with which he was intrusted was a private one, and could be delivered to himself only. The room was immediately cleared of all the inmates except Powhattan and his two wives, and then the emperor bade Hamor speak on.

Speaking through the medium of Savage, his interpreter, Hamor told Powhattan that Sir Thomas Dale had sent him a present of two pieces of copper, five strings of white and blue beads, five wooden combs, ten fish-hooks, and a couple of knives; and that when the emperor chose to send for it, he would also give him a grindstone. Thus far Powhattan expressed himself well pleased; but when Hamor told the emperor that his brother Dale, hearing of the fame of his youngest daughter, desired that she might be sent to the colony in charge of his messenger, both for a testimony of his love, and for the pleasure of her sister, Powhattan replied gravely:

"I gladly except from Sir Thomas Dale his salutations of love and peace, which while I live I will exactly keep. I also thank him for his presents, though they are fewer than has been customary; but for my daughter, I have already disposed of her hand, within a few days past, to a great Werowance, for two bushels of Roanoke."

Hamor instantly replied, that he knew very well it would not be difficult to revoke this arrangement, by returning the Roanoke, especially as the child was at that time but twelve years of age. He said it would have the further effect of gratifying Sir Thomas Dale, who would gladly bestow in return for the compliment, a present in beads, copper, hatchets, and other articles, worth at least three times as much as the Roanoke. The answer of Powhattan was as fatherly as it was direct and to the purpose.

"I love my daughter as my life, and though I have many children, I delight in none of them as much as I do in her, whom if I do not often behold I cannot possibly live. If she lived with you I should never be able to see her again, as I have resolved, upon no consideration, to place myself in your hands, or to come in person among you. Tell my brother, Sir Thomas Dale, that I desire no better assurance of his friendship than the promise he has made. One of my daughters is already a pledge for my good faith, which, so long as she lives, shall be sufficient. When she dies he shall have another. I do not think it the part of a brother to desire to bereave me of two daughters at once. Tell Sir Thomas Dale this. If he had no pledge whatever from me, he need fear no injury, either from myself or my people. There have been too many of his men and mine slain already, and with my consent there shall be no more; for I am old, and would gladly end my days in peace. If you offer me injury, my country is large enough for me to go from you. This I hope will satisfy my brother; and as you are weary, and I am sleepy, we will now end."

The Lady Rebecca Rolfe remained in the colony until 1616, when, in company with her husband and Sir Thomas Dale, she sailed for England. Through the unwearied diligence of John Rolfe, assisted by that meek and self-denying apostle of the wilderness, Alexander Whitaker, she had been taught to speak the English tongue, and to understand, though perhaps dimly, the more essential truths of Christianity. Happy in the enthusiastic love of her husband, she never expressed any desire to return to her father, and in the society of those of her own nation she no longer took any delight. When she left the shores of Virginia, her fame had already preceded her. Her presence was no sooner known in England, than all classes vied with each other in doing honour to the young wife and mother. On her way to London, many persons of rank and quality entertained her in a hospitable manner. The London Company took upon themselves the expenses of herself and child. The queen invited her to court, and Captain Smith evinced his gratitude to his preserver by writing a pamphlet expressly to exhibit the many and important services she had rendered to the colonists.

But she did not long enjoy these manifold honours. In less than one year after her arrival, at the age of twenty-two, she fell a victim to the English climate, just as she was on the eve of embarking at Gravesend for her native land.

CHAPTER X.

Evils arising from the system of common labour—Right of private property—Conditions of tenure—Indentured servants—Bounty land—Dale embarks for England—Appointment of Yeardley—Cultivation of tobacco—Careless security of the colonists—The savages taught the use of fire-arms—Argall supersedes Yeardley—His character and arbitrary conduct—His removal from office—Yeardley reappointed—Second administration of Yeardley—The first general assembly convened at Jamestown—How composed—Energy of Sandys—Large numbers of immigrants sent to Virginia—Importation of females—Beneficial effect upon the colonists—Rapid increase of immigrants—Introduction of negro slavery—Resignation of Sandys—His successor nominated by King James—Spirited conduct of the London Company—Earl of Southampton elected treasurer—The first constitution of Virginia.

DURING the period that the colonists were fed from the public stores, and all were alike compelled to labour for the common benefit, every excuse to avoid work was taken advantage of by the numerous idlers in the community; while such as were disposed to be industrious grew disheartened on finding themselves, at the end of each successive year, in no better condition than those who had systematically evaded all species of industry.

The beneficial effects of establishing the right of private property in lands soon displayed themselves, and proved, in the most emphatic manner, the wisdom of the measure. The conditions of tenure were, however, very unequal. Such of the colonists as had been sent over at the sole expense of the company received only three acres of land. Eleven months of each year they were required to work for the company, the other month they could employ as they thought fit. But this kind of enforced servitude soon grew out of favour, the number gradually decreased, and in 1617 there were of this description but fifty-four persons, of all ages, within the limits of the colony.

Those who farmed the plantations at the Bermudas hundreds fared much better. The settlers at this place paid annually into the public store but two barrels and a half of corn, and were not required to perform any more than one month's public service, which was not to be demanded of them either in seedtime or harvest.

During the earlier struggles of the colony, the bounty in land offered by the company to such as migrated to the new country at their own expense, or who had defrayed the cost of others, was one hundred acres for each person; but after the colony was more firmly established, the bounty was reduced to fifty acres, the actual occupancy and cultivation of which entitled the immigrant to claim fifty acres more. By a payment of twelve pounds ten shillings, each adventurer could obtain a grant of one hundred acres, and a claim to as much more as soon as the previous tract was settled and improved.

After remaining five years in the country, Sir Thomas Dale embarked for England in 1616, leaving the government in the hands of Sir George Yeardley.

The first articles of commerce, to the production of which the early settlers almost exclusively devoted themselves, were potash, soap, glass, and tar. Distance, however, and a want of the proper facilities to enable them to manufacture cheaply, rendered the cost of these commodities so great, that exports of a similar character from Russia and Sweden were still enabled to maintain their old ascendency in the markets of Europe. After many fruitless and costly experiments in the culture of the vine, the growing demand for tobacco enabled the planters to turn their labour into a profitable channel. As the demand increased the profits became correspondingly great, and every other species of labour was abandoned for the culture of tobacco. The houses were neglected, the palisades suffered to rot down, the fields, gardens, and public squares, even the very streets of Jamestown, were planted with tobacco. The townspeople, more greedy of gain than mindful of their own security, scattered abroad into the wilderness, where they broke up small pieces of rich ground and made their crops, regardless of their proximity to the Indians, in whose good faith so little reliance could be placed.

So imprudent were the colonists in this respect, that, encouraged by the example of the Deputy-governor Yeardley, they taught the savages the use of fire-arms, and employed them as hunters. It is true they were on good terms with all the surrounding tribes, but the danger to which this reckless mode of living exposed the colony was none the less imminent.

In May, 1619, Captain Samuel Argall superseded Yeardley, as deputy-governor of Virginia. This change of administration was by no means for the better. Argall was a stern arbitrary seaman, rugged and self-willed to a degree. Unfortunately, these ill qualities were not tempered, as is often the case in seamen, by generosity. Argall was appointed both military and naval commander in Virginia, and, as martial law was still in force, his power was despotic in the extreme. Had he exercised his authority with the same mildness and forbearance which characterized the acts of his predecessors, even though the laws were rigid and their mode of operation summary, it is not probable that the colonists would have preferred any cause of complaint. But Argall rendered his power subservient to his avarice, and sought, for his own selfish purposes, to make even innocent persons amenable to the severe military code. For a long time he succeeded in carrying on a system of exaction and extortion without rebuke. At length his avaricious grasp took a wider sweep. Not satisfied with confiscating to his own use the property of the colonists, he sought to increase his means by defrauding the company. These acts finally occasioned his deposition from office, and in 1619 Sir George Yeardley was appointed captain-general of the colony.

Before the latter arrived in Virginia, a pinnace had been despatched to the colony by the friends of Argall in London, to warn him of the charges which had been preferred against him, and of his removal from office. Argall at once made preparations for his own safety.

The pinnace reached Jamestown about the 1st of April, and within five days Argall set sail from the colony, leaving for his deputy Captain Nathaniel Powell. On the 18th of April, Sir George Yeardley reached Virginia, and informed the colonists of the favourable change which had taken place in the affairs of the London Company, and of the great supplies they were preparing to send out.

The administration of the new governor was as much distinguished by its gentleness and liberality as that of Argall's was for its tyranny and rapacity. The planters were released henceforth from all service to the colony, and were confirmed in their property, both personal and real, as amply as the subjects of England.

The removal of all restrictions upon labour, and the grant to the colonists of all the rights and privileges of freemen, mark the second period of Yeardley's administration as one of more than ordinary interest. Argall's impositions were denounced, the rigorous military code qualified and softened, and the English statute law gradually substituted in its stead. From this time there was no fear of scarcity, for food became so plentiful in the colony that the Indians, who formerly supplied a considerable portion of the corn consumed by the settlers, became occasional purchasers.

Self-interest, and the consciousness of enjoying a rational degree of liberty, and the right to dispose of their property in any manner they thought proper, incited every ambitious spirit to exert himself to the utmost. The demand for tobacco increased, the profits became enormous, and large sums were realized, as well by individuals as by the company, who had expended such a vast amount in sustaining a great project under so many and such serious discouragements.

The London Company, at this period, moved by an honourable spirit of liberality, rescinded nearly all their former colonial regulations, and substituted others of a far milder and more attractive character. The authority of the governor, which had latterly been despotic in the extreme, was now tempered and controlled by a council, who possessed the power to redress his errors. The colonists were also called upon to meet at Jamestown, and in a properly organized assembly assume the duties of local legislation.

This was almost exclusively the act of Yeardley. He convened at Jamestown, toward the close of June, 1619, the first colonial assembly that ever met in Virginia. It consisted of two burgesses from each of the eleven boroughs or corporations into which the colony was divided. Several acts were passed during the first session of this body, which, on being sent to England for ratification, were received with expressions of approval.

The scheme of colonization now proceeded rapidly. The affairs of the London Company were in the hands of a council possessing both energy and patriotism. Sir Edwin Sandys, the new treasurer, was a man whom neither lures nor threats could prevent from exposing the corruptions and abuses which had prevailed for so many years under the previous management. During twelve years, eighty thousand pounds had been expended by the company, and as yet the colony contained but six hundred persons.

In one year, Sandys provided a passage for twelve hundred and sixty-one immigrants, among whom were ninety young and incorrupt women, sent out as wives to such colonists as were matrimonially inclined. This importation of poor but virtuous girls was received with great favour. They were married either to the servants of the company, or to men well able to support them, and the cost of their transportation willingly defrayed.

The success which the first consignment met with induced the company to venture on a second. In 1621, sixty more were sent over, maids of virtuous education, young, handsome, and well recommended. The blessings of domestic life had already begun to be appreciated. The original cost of a wife was one hundred pounds of tobacco; but as the value of home enjoyments became better understood, the price of the members of the second consignment rose to one hundred and fifty pounds. It was an excellent and a thoughtful act. Hitherto Virginia had been regarded merely in the light of a temporary residence, where wealth was to be acquired more speedily than at home; but few thought of making the colony their permanent place of abode.

The formation of domestic attachments, the beauty of the climate, a personal interest in the soil, and the peaceful bearing of the surrounding Indians, gradually excited a desire in many to end their days in a land which offered a comfortable subsistence to ordinary industry, and numerous facilities for the rearing of a family.

Nothing tended so effectually to restrain the reckless spirit and unsettled habits of the colonists as the introduction of so many women among them. The debt for a wife was a debt of honour, and took precedence of any other. Married men were regarded by the company as the better and more reliable portion of the population, and favoured accordingly. The colony being now fixed upon a permanent basis, large numbers of immigrants flocked in. Within three years, fifty patents for land were granted, and three thousand five hundred persons left England for Virginia.

Great complaints having arisen in England against the governor and officers of the colony in regard to the use of covenanted and indented servants, instructions were issued by the council for the reformation of the existing abuses. One hundred men were allotted the governor to work on his plantation, free of charge, during the term of his administration. Fifty to the deputy-governor farming the college land; fifty to the deputy farming the company's land; fifty to the treasurer, and twenty-five to the secretary, and more to the marshal and cape merchant. On the retirement or removal of these officials, they were to make over an equal number of servants to their successors. The object of this generous distribution was to enable the officers of the com pany to acquire such a competency, as would permit them to live well without oppressing any under their charge.

But the event which exercised the most important influence upon the future condition of the colony was the introduction of African slaves.

In the month of August, 1620, the commander of a Dutch man-of-war entered James River, and disposed of twenty negroes. For a long time thereafter, this species of traffic progressed but slowly; so that, at the end of thirty years, the white population of Virginia outnumbered the black in the proportion of fifty to one.

The previous purchase of indented white servants, many of whom were kidnapped from their own country and sold among the planters for a term of years, made the transition from limited white to permanent negro slavery so simple and easy, as not only to create no compunctions of conscience, but to cause the change to be seriously regarded by many as taking the burden from the shoulders of their own countrymen, and placing it upon a race furnishing hereditary bondsmen from the remotest ages, and always regarded as forming the lowest type of humanity.

After serving as treasurer for the London Company for one year, the able and energetic Sandys resigned his office. The election of his successor was not effected without a severe contest. King James, jealous of the liberal and patriotic spirit in which the affairs of the company had lately been conducted, endeavoured to interfere. He nominated four candidates, from among whom the company were desired to choose their treasurer. Firm in upholding their rights, they successfully resisted the royal interference, rejected the nominees of the king, and made choice of the Earl of Southampton, the early patron of Shakspeare.

The subsequent proceedings of the company were equally just and humane. They emphatically repudiated the arbitrary conduct of Argall in a case of appeal from a sentence of death pronounced by him while acting in his capacity of governor. They discountenanced the opinion formerly prevailing that trial by martial law was the noblest kind of trial, and successfully asserted the rights of the colonists to trial by a jury of their peers.

The assembly of burgesses summoned by Yeardley was now formally sanctioned. In July, 1621, the company gave to the Virginians a written constitution, which guarantied to the colonists a much greater share of liberty than they had hitherto enjoyed.

Under the new form of government the governor and council of state for the colony were to be chosen by the treasurer, council, and company in England; and were to constitute a portion of the general assembly. The other members of the assembly were to consist of two burgesses from every town, hundred, or other particular plantation, to be chosen by the inhabitants themselves. This assembly, which was to be convened by the governor once a year, was to have full power to treat, consult, and conclude upon all subjects concerning the public welfare of the colony, and to enact such general laws and orders for the benefit of the colony, and the good government thereof, as from time to time might seem necessary. A negative voice was reserved to the governor; and the laws, to be rendered valid, were to receive the subsequent sanction of the London Company. As an equivalent concession to the colony, it was ordained, that after the new government shall have gone into operation, no orders of the court in London shall bind the colony unless ratified in like manner by the general assembly.

CHAPTER XI.

Sir Francis Wyatt appointed governor—Arrives in Virginia—Scattered condition of the colonists—Their careless state of security—Death of Powhattan—Opechancanough suspected of treachery—His answer—Arranges a plan for the general massacre of the colonists—Nemattanow, or Jack of the Feather, murders one Morgan and robs him—Is shot down by two boys—His dying requests—Terrible massacre of the 22d of March—Most of the plantations abandoned—Sickness in the colony—War of extermination—Reception of the tidings in England—Assistance sent to the colonists—Smith tenders his services—Conduct of King James—Attempts to dictate to the company—Meets with a second rebuke—Resolves to annul the charter—Appoints commissioners to inquire into the affairs of the company—Resolves to reassume his conceded authority—His proposition rejected by the company—Commissioners sent to Virginia.

As the term of office for which Sir George Yeardley was appointed drew near to a close, the council in London made choice of Sir Francis Wyatt to succeed him. The latter, with nine ships freighted with immigrants and supplies, reached Virginia in October, 1621. A part of his instructions was to raise less tobacco and more corn. He found the colonists dispersed in small parties, widely separated; their plantations extending along the James River, and toward the Potomac, wherever the richest land could be found. Increase of numbers had made them carelessly secure. Many of them lived familiarly among the savages; slept with them in their houses, employed them as hunters, and took no pains to guard themselves from surprise.

The aged Emperor Powhattan died in 1618, gratefully reverenced by his own people, and honoured by his English neighbours. From the period of his daughter's marriage until that of his own decease, he remained the firm and steadfast friend of the colonists. He was succeeded by his younger brother Itopatin, but the more daring spirit of Opechancanough soon led him to usurp the imperial authority. Although this change, from the known character of Opechancanough, rendered a continuance of amicable relations doubtful and uncertain, the colonists, confident in their numbers, neglected the most ordinary precautions. One reason for this may have been their consciousness that the number of Indians occupying each village was but small; that these villages were widely scattered along the banks of the various rivers between the James and the Potomac, and that the whole savage population, within sixty miles of Jamestown, did not number more than five thousand souls, of whom some fifteen hundred only were warriors. The eastern shore Indians never occasioned the English any trouble whatever, but even under occasional circumstances of great provocation, always remained peaceful and well-disposed. Some floating rumour that Opechancanough intended to prove treacherous, led Wyatt, about the middle of March, 1622, to send an envoy to him, for the purpose of renewing the treaty which had been made with his predecessors.

Opechancanough received the messenger with the greatest respect, and confirmed the treaty not only with alacrity and cheerfulness, but accompanied the act with many expressions of good-will. He told the messenger that he held the peace so firm, that the sky should fall before he would violate it. At this very time he was perfecting his schemes for a general massacre, which only failed in entire success from the affection which one of his own people bore to a colonist who had befriended him.

So well arranged were all the preliminaries of the plot, and so faithfully had the secret been preserved, that only two days before the massacre, the Indians guided the English through the forest as usual, and even borrowed boats of the colonists to cross the river and consult with their friends upon the sanguinary measures they were about to undertake. On the evening of Thursday, and even on the morning of Friday, the 22d of March, the very day on which the massacre was appointed to take place, they came unarmed into the houses of the English, under pretence of bringing game and other provisions for sale, and in some instances sat down to breakfast with their destined victims.

One of the prominent pretexts by which Opechancanough had stimulated his people to combine together, and by a simultaneous attack upon all the English settlements, to exterminate the intruders at a single unexpected blow, was to avenge the death of a favourite warrior by the name of Nemattanow.

This Nemattanow was held in great esteem by the Indians generally. As he had been engaged in many conflicts and escaped unhurt, they believed him to be invulnerable. Taking advantage of their credulity, he affected a marked singularity of dress and demeanour; making everywhere an open boast of his person being proof against all kinds of warlike weapons. By his strange ways, and fantastic style of wearing feather ornaments, he obtained among the English the nickname of Jack of the Feather.

Nemattanow, being desirous of possessing some toys and gewgaws, belonging to one Morgan, went to his house and persuaded the latter to accompany him to Pamunkey, where he asserted they could be disposed of to great advantage. Morgan consented, and Nemattanow murdered and robbed him by the way. Two days afterward, he boldly returned to Morgan's house, wearing on his head the cap of the dead man. Here he found two well-grown boys that had been hired to Morgan, who immediately asked where their master was. He told them he was dead, but refusing to give them any further particulars, they demanded he should go with them before a magistrate, and relate all he knew concerning Morgan's mysterious disappearance. As Nemattanow not only declined going, but commenced insolently abusing them, they shot him down, and then placed him in a boat, intending to carry him before the governor, at that time some seven or eight miles from them. The wound Nemattanow had received proving mortal, he earnestly entreated the boys in his last moments to promise him two things; the one was, that they would not make it known in what manner he had been killed; and the other, that they would bury him among the English.

When the loss of Nemattanow was made known to Opechancanough, he broke out into such threats of revenge as induced Wyatt to send the messenger to him, whose conference with the great chieftain resulted in renewed and solemn assurances of his desire to remain at peace.

It has been already stated, that the preparations for the massacre were made with the utmost secrecy. At mid-day on the 22d of March, the savages, having marched out from their numerous villages, posted themselves, as by previous concert, in or near the various settlements of the English, and fell upon them suddenly at one and the same moment of time. The attack was so immediate and unsuspected, that in numerous instances not the least resistance was offered. Some had entered the houses under pretence of trading; others bearing presents of game and fish; others again mingled with the labourers in the fields with the familiarity of friends; while the more cautious settlers were enticed abroad under various and apparently plausible pretexts. Whenever the Indians obtained the mastery, they spared none, but destroyed man, woman, and child. Those whom they knew to be friends shared the same fate as their bitterest enemies. Even the pure and single-hearted missionaries, who had always mixed with them freely, and sought to win their regard by unwearying acts of kindness, even they too were murdered, and their bodies mutilated in all those hideous and horrible ways which only savage barbarity could devise.

And yet these bloodthirsty men were as cowardly as they were treacherous and sanguinary. Whenever any resistance was offered they fled. The firing of a single musket, the mere lifting of an axe or a hatchet, was in many instances sufficient to divert them from their purpose, and hurry them away from a place that was even slightly defended, to attack another the inhabitants of which were more timid or less prepared. All they could massacre by surprise during that day fell victims to their fury. With the setting of the sun the slaughter ended, and satiated with blood the Indians retired toward their several villages. On that fatal morning, three hundred and forty-seven persons were cut off, most of them falling by their own weapons, or implements of industry.

But Jamestown, and the settlements immediately surrounding it, were providentially saved. Only one of all the Indians who were privy to the conspiracy cherished a sufficiently grateful remembrance of the favours he had received, to enable him to overcome the repugnance he experienced at betraying the cherished secret which had been confided to his people.

Two Indians, who were brothers, chanced to sleep together the night previous to the massacre at the house of a man named Pace, by whom one of the brothers was employed. The other Indian, who was in the employ of another planter named Perry, urged upon his brother to rise and kill Pace at once, and confided to him the whole plot, which was to be executed on the morrow. The Indian in the service of Pace consented to do as he was bid, and immediately went out, leaving his brother under the impression that he had quitted him for the purpose of committing the murder.

Entering his master's chamber, he revealed to him the whole story. Pace instantly arose, and, after securing his house, rowed under cover of the darkness to Jamestown, and informed the governor what he had heard. By this means the capital of the colony, and such plantations as could receive the tidings in time to prepare for a defence, were preserved from the assault of the savages, who, on no single occasion, persevered in carrying out their bloody designs where they found the English in readiness to receive them, or where any thing approaching a sturdy resistance was offered.

The larger part of the colony was fortunately saved. A year after the massacre there still remained two thousand five hundred men; but the high-wrought sense of danger which led the colonists to abandon their plantations, for some time afterward seriously retarded their prosperity. Of eighty plantations which extended over a space of one hundred and forty miles on both sides of the James River, only eight were retained. Into these few the alarmed settlers congregated. The college lands were abandoned; the manufactories closed, and the culture of the fields limited to so confined a space as barely to afford the means for subsistence. Thus crowded together, sickness ensued, and some of the colonists, taking a sudden disgust to the country, abandoned it and returned to England. For some time, in the midst of the general consternation, none thought of retaliating the injuries they had sustained; but when grief and fear subsided, a war of extermination commenced.

In July of the following year, three hundred men penetrated to the Indian villages, and burned many of them; but the inhabitants invariably fled as they approached, and secreted themselves in the woods. After a fruitless pursuit, prolonged through several months, the English returned to their homes.

But the spirit of the people was thoroughly aroused. The gauntlet which had been thrown down by the Indians was now deliberately taken up, their property seized wherever it could be found, their plantations and villages sequestered, and, meeting guile with guile, even treachery was employed to bring their enemies into their hands.

In July, 1624, the general assembly ordered a foray similar to that which had taken place the year previous. This fierce but desultory warfare was continued for the space of ten years. The Indians were everywhere routed from their old habitations, and compelled to retreat before the footsteps of their relentless pursuers, deeper and deeper into the recesses of the forest.

When the tidings of the massacre were received in England, it created a profound sensation. Many of the adventurers grew despondent at their great losses, and parted with their shares for whatever they would bring. Others, however, were found ready to fill their places. A strong feeling of compassion for the struggling and unfortunate colony took possession of the national mind. Several gentlemen went over with their own servants and food, designing to take up the bounty lands offered to actual settlers. Others purchased grants of the company in London, and obtained authorities and jurisdictions separate from the colonial government. The latter was an evil policy on the part of the company, and one that subsequently led to disorders in the colony which threatened to involve it in the horrors of civil war.

The company despatched supplies and assistance. Even James affected a generosity he was incapable of feeling, and ordered from the Tower supplies of arms which he knew at the time to be utterly worthless. The city of London contributed to repair the losses of the Virginians. Smith, always ready to make a tender of his services wheresoever they might be useful, volunteered to keep the savages in subjection with a force of one hundred soldiers and thirty seamen; but from a want of funds on the part of the company, his project was not entertained. The only answer he could get was, that the charge would be too great, but that he could obtain permission to undertake it at his own cost, provided he would bestow upon the corporation one half of the pillage.

Taking advantage of the unfortunate condition in which the affairs of the company were now placed, King James, who had long been desirous of exercising control over the colony, sought the present opportunity to annul the charter, by fomenting dissensions among the adventurers.

The want of success which had hitherto attended the exertions of the company had led to much dissatisfaction among many of those who had for a long time held shares of stock so utterly unproductive. The company at this time consisted of a thousand adventurers, of whom some two hundred usually attended the quarter courts, where the undaunted advocacy of the principles of liberty was peculiarly obnoxious to the king, and to those adventurers who, being opposed to the patriotic party, found themselves in the minority, and could only hope to acquire the power they coveted by assisting the king to recover that control over the colony which he had already conceded by charter.

Desirous of gaining his ends by secret rather than open means, James exerted all his influence with the malcontents. When the meeting for a new choice of officers took place in 1622, he again intimated his desire that the treasurer of the company should be selected from one of the candidates whose names he had sent in. The company indignantly rebuked all interference with their chartered rights. They re-elected the Earl of Southampton treasurer by a large majority; only eight votes out of seventy being cast in favour of the candidates nominated by the king.

Finding it impossible to control the company through the means of its members, James resolved to annul the charter. He immediately sought a plausible pretext to do so without a too glaring violation of the laws of the realm. The malcontent members were easily prevailed upon to present two petitions to the king, setting forth the many evils which had befallen the colony, and attributing them to gross mismanagement on the part of the dominant members of the company. These charges contained some truths, mixed up with many falsehoods. Although they had been prepared with great secrecy, the company succeeded in obtaining copies, justified their course in the main by an able vindication, and supported their positions by testimony of a character too respectable to be controverted.

The king, being resolved to admit of no justification, appointed a commissioner to investigate the concerns of the company from its earliest settlement. The records were seized. The deputy-treasurer was imprisoned, and even private letters from Virginia were intercepted and broken open.

The report of the commissioners, as might have been expected, was favourable to the views of the king. In October, 1623, by an order in council, he declared the misfortunes of Virginia to have arisen from the mismanagement of the company, and that he had resolved by a new charter to reassume the appointment of a governor and assistants to reside in England; the power to negative similar appointments in Virginia, and the supreme control in colonial affairs. If the company resisted this change, its patent was to be annulled.

A proposition so entirely unexpected struck the company with amazement. Three several times the order in council was read, and no man uttered a word. At length the vote was taken, the result of which, by an overwhelming majority, was to stand by their charter.

They now craved a month's delay, in order that, by having a larger number of members present, they might be better able to come to a final decision. The privy council demanded a decisive answer should be sent in within three days. An extraordinary court was immediately summoned, and the resolution was carried, by a vote of sixty-three to seven, to defend the integrity of the patent.

This decision was probably expected. Four days afterward the king despatched five commissioners to Virginia, to inquire into all matters which concerned the interests of the colony, and orders were at the same time sent to the governor and council to render the committee all possible assistance.

CHAPTER XII.

Arrival of commissioners in Virginia—Feeling of the colonists—Proceedings of the commissioners—Pory suborns the clerk of the council—Punishment of the latter—The presence of the commissioners disregarded—Acts passed by the assembly—Taxation asserted to be dependent on representation—Regulations adopted to guard against surprise by the Indians—Charter of the London Company cancelled—Death of James I.—Great influx of immigrants—No towns in Virginia—Yeardley appointed governor—Lord Baltimore arrives in Virginia—Religious intolerance of the colonists—Baltimore returns to England—Obtains a patent for the province of Maryland—Yeardley succeeded by Sir John Harvey—Variance of opinions concerning the latter—He is deposed and sent to England—Is returned—Second Virginia massacre—Opechancanough taken prisoner—His death.

The commissioners appointed by James reached Virginia in the early part of the year 1624. At first, the colonists, taking but little interest in the controversy between the king and the company, were disposed to remain neutral; being contented, so long as their own rights were not invaded, to look quietly on; but when they had obtained, by means of secret friends in London, copies of the two petitions presented to the king, in which their country and condition were falsely represented, they met in general assembly, and returned a spirited reply in defence of their own honour and good name. A petition to the king was soon after drafted, and a member of the council sent to England, at the general charge of the colonists, to represent their interests. The chief prayer of the petition was, "that the governors may not have absolute power, and that they might still retain the liberty of popular assemblies, than which, nothing could more conduce to the public satisfaction and public utility."

Differences between the commissioners and the assembly soon occurred. As the former declined to make known the authority under which they acted, and the secret instructions with which they had been charged, the governor and assembly thought proper to preserve an equal mystery in regard to their own proceedings. With a view to obtain the information they required, Pory, one of the commissioners, now suborned the clerk of the council, and gained from him a full knowledge of the secret consultations of the Virginians. Indignant at this base treachery, the faithless clerk was promptly arrested and punished with the loss of his ears. After being thus baffled and exposed, the commissioners endeavoured, by alternate threats and promises, to induce the assembly to petition the crown for a revocation of the charter. In this they were equally unsuccessful.

The assembly, refusing to accredit men who declined to show the commission under which they acted, continued to legislate for the colony in their customary manner.

The acts passed at this period show that the colonists were fully sensible of their rights as a free and independent people. One act is peculiarly significant; it declares in the clearest language that taxation and representation must go together. This bold proposition is expressed in the following words: "The governor shall not lay any taxes or impositions upon the colonists, their lands, or commodities, in any other way than by the authority of the general assembly, to be levied and employed as the said assembly shall appoint."

To guard against any future surprise by the Indians, the most stringent regulations were adopted. There being but few of the inhabitants residing in towns, nearly all the colonists being scattered widely apart among the plantations, it was ordered that every house should be fortified with palisadoes, that no man should go or send abroad without a party sufficiently armed, or work in the fields without a sentry to keep guard over the arms. The inhabitants were forbidden to go aboard ships, or elsewhere, in such numbers as to endanger the safety of their plantations. Every planter was required to be provided with a sufficient quantity of arms and ammunition, to keep a strict watch by night, and to suffer no powder to be expended in amusement or entertainment. Corn planting was promoted by not restricting its price, and trade with the savages for that necessary article of food strictly prohibited.

Shortly after sending commissioners to Virginia, the king had caused a quo warranto to be issued against the company. The cause came up for trial during Trinity term, in 1624. It was, doubtless, already prejudged. Before the end of the term a judgment was declared by the Lord Chief Justice Ley against the company, and its charter cancelled.

On the return of the commissioners to England, they reported favourably of the soil and climate of Virginia, but censured deeply the conduct of the company. The dissolution of the latter was followed by no very general regret. It had been long engaged in bitter controversies, which crippled its influence, and abstracted greatly from its ability to answer the ends for which it had been originally organized. Its fall created no immediate change in the condition of the colony.

Sir Francis Wyatt was confirmed in his office, and himself and council only authorized to govern within the same limits as any previous governor and council resident there within the space of the five previous years.

The council nominated by the king was chosen with more than his usual wisdom; the selection being made from men of moderately liberal views in preference to violent court partisans.

The death of James, in March, 1625, put a stop to a project he had formed of framing a code of fundamental laws for the colony. He was succeeded by his son Charles I.

The prosperity of the colony steadily increased. Large numbers of immigrants sailed for the favoured country, where they took up land and settled separately on their plantations.

The passion for becoming owners of large tracts of land, combined with the advantages which the numerous rivers afforded for the shipment of tobacco from private wharves, encouraged a straggling system of settlement, which so effectually prevented the growth of towns, that eighty years after this period, or so late as 1703, there was not congregated together, in any one place in Virginia, a sufficient number of inhabitants to entitle the collection of houses to any higher rank than that of a small village.

Although Virginia had become a royal province, her rights and privileges were not interfered with by Charles. The latter was too intent upon monopolizing the trade in tobacco exported from the colony to inquire into the origin of its local legislation.

In 1626, Wyatt was succeeded as governor by Sir George Yeardley. No appointment could have been more satisfactory to the Virginians, as it relieved them from all fear that their form of government would undergo any radical change.

Charles had, doubtless, no design to take from the colonists their cherished privilege of self-government, and in the commission of the newly-appointed governor, expressly declared his wish to benefit, encourage, and perfect the colony, and to continue its prosperity by the same means that were formerly thought best suited to effect that purpose.

The colonial assembly was thus tacitly acknowledged; and as Yeardley had the honour of its first introduction, his reappointment was regarded as a happy omen.

The death of Yeardley, in 1628, led to the appointment of Sir John Harvey. During the interim, Francis West was elected by the council to occupy the office vacated by the decease of Yeardley, until his successor should arrive.

It was at this period that Lord Baltimore visited Virginia. His intention was to have settled in the colony, but having become by conviction a Roman Catholic, he was received with the utmost coldness by the people, who required him, as a preliminary to his becoming a recognised citizen of the colony, to take the oath of allegiance and supremacy. His religious scruples prevented him from complying with this demand, and, pained at the religious intolerance of which he had been made a striking example, he resolved upon seeking a settlement elsewhere.

With this view he explored the Chesapeake

Bay, and finding it as yet altogether uninhabited by the English, none of whose settlements extended beyond the south side of the Potomac River, he projected the plan of a new colony, to be founded under his own auspices, and entirely independent of Virginia. On his return to England, he succeeded in obtaining from Charles I. a grant of the province of Maryland, bounded to the south, on the western shore, by the Potomac River; and on the eastern shore, by an east line from Point Lookout. Lord Baltimore dying before his project was fully perfected, his son obtained, in 1633, a confirmation of the patent, and went over in person to plant his new colony.

On the unexpected return of West to England, John Pott was chosen Governor of Virginia, whose term of administration came to an end, in the autumn of 1629, by the arrival from England of Sir John Harvey.

The administration of Harvey has been variously characterized. By some historians he is regarded as having acted in a rapacious and tyrannical manner. His deposition from office in 1635, and his shipment to England, accompanied by commissioners empowered to lay their complaints before the king, gave a plausible colouring to the charge. On the other hand, his apologists point out the circumscribed power of the governor, and ask how it was possible for tyranny to have been exercised under a prerogative so limited?

There is very little doubt that the period during which Harvey was governor was one of great party heat and excitement.

A grant issued in 1630 to Sir Robert Heath, for the territory of South Carolina, was well calculated to produce an unpleasant state of feeling in Virginia, which the subsequent grant of Maryland to Lord Baltimore by no means tended to allay. The Virginians felt that the boundaries of their province had been unjustly circumscribed, and they charged Harvey with having rendered assistance in obtaining the obnoxious patents.

That the colonists must have felt themselves seriously aggrieved before they ventured upon an act, than which nothing was more likely to draw upon them the displeasure of the king, cannot be doubted for a moment. Charles was indeed indignant. He refused to hear the commissioners, sent them directly home, and reinstated Harvey in his former office without instituting any inquiry into his previous conduct.

In 1639, Harvey was succeeded by Sir Francis Wyatt. The latter remained in office only two years, when he surrendered his authority into the hands of Sir William Berkeley.

During the earlier years of Berkeley's administration, many new and judicious laws were made by the Virginians, which tended to perfect their system of government. Condemnations to service were abolished, the courts of justice made more conformable to those of England, religion was provided for, the land titles adjusted, and the boundary difficulties with Maryland amicably arranged.

The contending factions by which England was at this time torn did not in any serious degree affect Virginia. There, all was peace, concert, and harmony. The Indians, against whom inroads were made almost annually, having heard of the troubles in the mother country, were instigated by the now very aged Opechancanough to cut off, by a second massacre, three hundred of the colonists. The loss fell severest upon the plantations to the south of James River, and on the heads of the other rivers, but chiefly in the neighbourhood of the Pamunkey, where the authority of Opechancanough was most implicitly recognised.

Opechancanough had been in his earlier years a man of large stature and of commanding appearance. He has been called, by Smith and other historians, the brother of Powhattan; but the tradition of the Indians was different. They spoke of him as a prince of a foreign nation, who came to them a great way from the south-west; and from accounts subsequently given to the settlers, he was supposed to have sprung from the Spanish Indians on the frontiers of Mexico. One thing is certain, whether a native or a foreign prince, from the first settlement of Jamestown until his own death, he continued either secretly or openly the bitter foe to the English.

No sooner did the tidings of this massacre reach Berkeley, than he commenced against the savages retaliatory measures of the severest kind. Their villages were burned to the ground, their crops destroyed, and they themselves, hunted incessantly among the recesses of the forest, were shot down without mercy wherever they could be found. The aged Opechancanough was the especial object of pursuit. He had now grown so decrepit, that, being unable to walk alone, he was carried by his men wherever he was compelled to flee before his relentless pursuers. His once stalwart person was now gaunt and emaciated. His sinews slackened, and his eyelids had become so heavy that he could not see but as they were lifted up by his servants. In this low condition he was surprised in his hiding-place by a party of horse, and conducted a prisoner to Jamestown. He was received by the governor with all respect and tenderness, but he did not survive his capture more than two weeks; one of the soldiers by whom he was taken prisoner having basely shot him through the back, in revenge for the injuries which the colonists had suffered.

He bore up with stoical bravery to the last moment of his life, and did not exhibit the least dejection at his captivity. Hearing one day the sound of numerous footsteps about him, he caused his eyelids to be lifted, and finding that a crowd of persons had been admitted to see him, he called indignantly for the governor, and told him with great scorn, that if it had been his fortune to have taken Sir William Berkeley prisoner, he would not meanly have exposed him as a show to the people. The mortified chieftain had forgotten the exultation with which, at an earlier day, he had paraded Virginia's noblest champion, Captain John Smith, through all the Indian villages from the Pamunkey to the Potomac.

CHAPTER XIII.

Berkeley sails for England—Treaty of peace with the Indians—Prosperity of Virginia—Her loyalty—Hospitality extended to fugitive Cavaliers—Charles II. proclaimed—Action of the English Parliament—Virginia acknowledges the commonwealth—Berkeley resigns—Richard Bennett elected governor—Indian incursion—Edward Diggs elected governor—Samuel Matthews chosen governor—His controversy with the burgesses—Declares the dissolution of the assembly—The assembly deposes the governor and council—Re-elects Matthews—His submission—Richard Cromwell—Acknowledged protector of England—The Virginia assembly defines its privileges—Restoration of Charles II.—Berkeley sails for England—The laws of Virginia revised.

The prosperity of the province of Virginia suffered no material check from the last Indian outbreak. The savages themselves were alarmed at their own temerity, and, to avoid the wrath they had provoked, fled immediately from the scene of massacre. The settlers most exposed upon the frontiers banded together for self-defence during a brief period; but even then companies of ten men were considered sufficient to insure protection against any force which the savages could bring against them.

In June, 1644, Berkeley sailed for England. During his absence, Richard Kemp was elected by the council to exercise the functions of governor.

Berkeley returned to the province in June, 1645, and reassumed the duties of his office. In October of the following year, a treaty of peace was concluded with Necotowance, the successor of Opechancanough. By the terms of this treaty, the Indians were permitted to inhabit the north side of the York or Pamunkey River, while the whites obtained a cession, for ever, of all the country from the falls of the James and York to the Chesapeake Bay.

The long struggle between Charles I. and the Parliament, which ended in the decapitation of the king, and the elevation of Oliver Cromwell to the protectorate, crowded the ports of Virginia with vessels and immigrants. At the close of 1648, thirty-one ships traded to the province, twelve of which were from London and Bristol, a like number from Holland, and seven from New England.

Attached to the cause of Charles from the moderation with which he had exercised his prerogative as regarded themselves, the Virginians were disposed to look upon the success of the parliamentary party in England as likely to affect the welfare of the province injuriously. Such fugitive Cavaliers, therefore, as sought a home among them, they welcomed with the most unbounded hospitality. Every house was a shelter for them, and every planter a friend.

Berkeley, also a devoted loyalist, received the

fugitives with open arms. His purse and his dwelling were free to all. Charles II. was proclaimed with enthusiasm the rightful monarch of Virginia, and every expression of dissent on the part of the few republicans who inclined to the cause of the English commonwealth was promptly rebuked.

Charles, then an exile at Breda, did not fail to evince his gratification at the loyalty displayed by Virginia. He sent Berkeley a renewal of his commission as governor, and suggested fit candidates for various offices in the province.

For three years after the execution of Charles I., the authority of his son was acknowledged by Virginia.

No sooner, however, were affairs tranquillized nearer home, than the English Parliament turned its attention to the colonies. An ordinance was passed empowering the council of state to reduce the rebellious colonies to obedience, and closing the ports of Barbadoes, Antigua, Bermudas, and Virginia, against foreign trading vessels. Maryland had already made submission, and Massachusetts, anticipating the orders of Parliament, to preserve the independence of her own legislation, had prohibited all intercourse with Virginia until the supremacy of the commonwealth should be established.

In the early part of 1652, an English squadron, after reducing Antigua and Barbadoes, entered the waters of the Chesapeake. Active preparations had previously been made by the Virginians for a vigorous defence; but when terms were offered them, by which it was agreed that the act of submission should be considered a voluntary one, and not enforced by conquest; that they should enjoy equal liberty with the free-born people of England; that they should enact their own laws by general assembly as hitherto; and that they should be free from all taxes, customs, and impositions whatever, except such as the general assembly should consent to, there was no longer any reason or policy to persevere in their resistance, and therefore, upon those terms, the articles of surrender were signed by the general assembly and the commissioners of the commonwealth.

By this amicable arrangement, Virginia lost nothing of her former independence. Berkeley, a devoted loyalist, immediately resigned his office, and Richard Bennett, one of the commissioners, was elected governor. A new council was also organized, with power to act only upon such instructions from England as should be first ratified by the general assembly. At the same session it was declared best that officers should be elected by the burgesses, who were the representatives of the people, and the governor and council were only to be admitted in future to seats in the assembly, by taking a similar oath to that required of the burgesses.

About this time the colony was again troubled with Indian hostilities. A number of strange Indians, calling themselves Rechahecrians, descended from their homes among the mountains, to the number of six or seven hundred warriors, and took up a strong position on the falls of James River. The first expedition sent against them returned unsuccessful. A second one was organized soon after, which was accompanied by a band of tributary Indians under their chief Totopotomoi. Supported by the English, these savage allies fought with desperate bravery. They numbered one hundred men; and were nearly all of them killed, including their chief.

In 1655, Edward Diggs, who, as a member of the council, had given repeated proofs of his fidelity to Virginia and the commonwealth of England, was elected governor by the assembly.

In March, 1658, the choice of the assembly fell upon "worthy Samuel Matthews, an old planter of forty years standing, who kept a good house, lived bravely, and was a true lover of Virginia."

Notwithstanding this high praise of Governor Matthews, his elevation appears to have inspired him with so exalted an idea of his prerogative as to lead him into a controversy with the assembly. The latter had extended its powers by making a change in the constitution, under which all laws were in future to be discussed in private session, and not, as heretofore, in the presence of the governor and his council. Instead also of dissolving the assembly, the burgesses thought fit to adjourn the session until November.

On the 1st of April, the governor and council declared by message a dissolution of the assembly. The answer of the latter denied the legality of the act, and requested that it should be revoked. A resolution was then carried, by which such members as separated from the rest of the assembly were to incur censure as false to the trust reposed in them, and the acts of those remaining were to be considered as the acts of the entire house. Each member was further bound, by oath, not to disclose the proceedings of the assembly.

This sturdy resistance to the dictation of the governor induced him to yield; but as he expressed, at the same time, his intention to appeal to the protector, the assembly voted his answer unsatisfactory, and requested him to revoke his order of dissolution.

Matthews consented to do so, but still asserted his determination to refer the dispute to Cromwell for his decision.

Fully conscious that such an act would be likely to jeopardize their liberties, the members of the assembly resolved on a solemn assertion of their independent powers. They declared the house of burgesses incapable of dissolution by any authority in Virginia except their own. To show that they possessed the right to remove obnoxious officers, they deposed the governor and council, and then re-elected the former and a part of the latter. They further resolved, that in future no one should be admitted of the council unless he was nominated, appointed, and confirmed by the house of burgesses.

These bold proceedings effectually alarmed Matthews. He consented to hold his office on their own terms, and acknowledged the supremacy of the assembly by taking the new oath which they prescribed. The principle of popular sovereignty being thus unequivocally admitted, the public business was conducted in future with the utmost harmony.

When Cromwell died, in March, 1659, the burgesses, after deliberating privately, unanimously resolved to recognise his son Richard.

As the council in England, in the letter which officially notified to the Virginians the death of the protector, had left their government to be conducted according to former usage, the assembly determined to define its existing powers in the most explicit manner.

The governor was accordingly summoned to attend the house, and in the presence of the whole assembly, to solemnly acknowledge that the supreme power of electing officers was by the present laws resident in the grand assembly.

The reason assigned for requiring this submissive avowal on the part of the governor affords a remarkable evidence of the estimation in which the Virginians held their popular sovereignty. It was, in order "that what was their privilege now, might be the privilege of their posterity."

The protectorate of Richard Cromwell was speedily brought to an end by his quiet resignation of an authority which he had no ambition to wield.

About the same time, Governor Matthews died. The burgesses were immediately called together. As England was without an acknowledged head, they decreed that the supreme power of Virginia should be vested in the assembly, and that all writs should issue in its name until a commission, recognised as legal by the assembly itself, should arrive from England.

Sir William Berkeley, who had resided quietly upon his plantation during the protectorate of Cromwell, was now re-elected governor. He consented to accept the office at the hands of the assembly, acknowledged himself its servant, agreed to call an assembly once in two years at least, and not to dissolve it without its own consent.

But while thus tenacious of their liberties, the Virginians felt no desire to be released from their allegiance to England so long as they were permitted to retain the power of controlling their own affairs. Notwithstanding their politic recognition of the English commonwealth, their loyalty to the Stuarts remained unshaken.

During the interregnum, Virginia regulated her own commerce by acts of independent legislation. She opened her ports to all foreign ships, on the payment of no higher duty than was levied on English vessels bound to a foreign port; she entertained proposals of peace and commerce with New Netherlands; and extended, by special statute, to every Christian nation at peace with England, a promise of liberty to trade and equal justice.

Upon the restoration of Charles II., the latter sent Berkeley a new commission, with leave to return to England, and power to appoint a deputy in his absence. Leaving Colonel Francis Morrison deputy-governor, Berkeley set sail, and was received by the king with great kindness. The attachment of Charles to the most loyal of his colonies is well known. Tradition states, that in compliment to the province of Virginia, he wore at his coronation a robe made of the silk sent from thence; but the affection of the restored monarch never subsequently displayed itself in any more substantial manner.

While Berkeley was absent, Colonel Morrison, acting under the instructions of his superior, revised the laws of Virginia, and compiled them into one body, ready to be confirmed by the assembly on his return. By these laws the church of England was recognised as the established religion; the change of the government sustained, trade and manufactures encouraged, a town projected, and all Indian affairs settled.

The parishes were likewise regulated. Competent allowances of about eighty pounds a year, besides glebes and perquisites, were made to ministers. Their method of preferment was also adjusted, convenient churches and glebes were provided, and all necessary parish officers instituted. Some steps were also made toward establishing a free school and a college, and all the poor were effectually provided for.

For the support of the government, the duty of two shillings on each hogshead of tobacco, and one shilling on every ton of shipping, was made perpetual, and the collectors rendered responsible for the same to the general assembly.

For the encouragement of manufactures, bounties were offered for the best pieces of linen and woollen cloth, and fifty pounds of tobacco were offered for each pound of silk. All persons were enjoined to plant mulberry trees in proportion to the number of acres they held. Tanneries were erected in each county at the county charge, and public encouragement given to a salt-work on the eastern shore. A bounty was also offered in proportion to tonnage for all ships built in the province, which were also to be exempted from all the customary fees and duties.

CHAPTER XIV.

Jamestown in 1662—Increase of nonconformists—Persecution of—Their migration from Virginia—Projected massacre—Its opportune discovery—The prosperity of the province checked by injurious English laws—Futile attempts of the assembly to remedy the evil—An exploring party cross the Blue Ridge—Growing difficulties—Change in the political condition of the Virginians—Statistics of the province in 1671—Oppressed situation of the poorer planters—Magnificent vagaries of Charles II.—Agents sent to England—Popular disturbances—Descent of the Seneca Indians upon the Susquehannas—Outrages committed on the frontiers by the latter—Six chiefs treacherously murdered—Sanguinary retaliation—Arming of the Virginians—Berkeley reprobates war—Nathaniel Bacon—His condition and character—Marches against the Indians.

ON his return from England in the latter part of the year 1662, Berkeley prevailed upon the assembly to pass an act for the improvement of Jamestown, which had dwindled into an insignificant village. Seventeen houses were accordingly erected therein at the expense of the several counties, who were allowed to impress labourers for the work at established rates. Every private person who built a house within the limits of the city was entitled to receive, as a bonus, from the public treasury, ten thousand pounds of tobacco.

All persons who consented to become citizens of the town were to be privileged from arrest for two years; all ships trading to Virginia were ordered to go to Jamestown and enter their cargoes before they broke bulk; and all tobacco made in the three neighbouring counties was directed to be brought to the same point and stored for shipment.

These regulations were soon found impracticable, and the assembly gave permission to such ships as were bound to the York, Rappahannock, and Potomac Rivers, to ride dispersed and anchor wherever it was found most convenient. Jamestown accordingly was but little increased in population under the new law which had been passed for its especial benefit, and for many years afterward consisted of but thirty-two brick houses, most of which were converted into taverns and other places of entertainment.

In 1663, the number of nonconformists increasing rapidly, the assembly, in order to check what it considered a growing evil, enacted that all who refused, "out of averseness to the orthodox established religion, or the new-fangled conceits of their own heretical inventions, to have their children baptized by the lawful minister, should be subjected to a fine of two thousand pounds of tobacco."

Other restraints and penalties, equally severe, being imposed upon those who could not in conscience conform to the doctrines of the church of England, many of them migrated into the neighbouring colonies, while others settled on the banks of the Chowan, where a few immigrants of the same persuasion had laid the foundation of what was subsequently to be known as the province of North Carolina.

This rigorous religious persecution, joined to the extremely low price of the staple commodity, tobacco, occasioned the poorer class of people to break out into loud murmurs against the government, and led to the formation of a conspiracy among the indented servants, some of whom had been soldiers under Cromwell. These latter, depending upon the malcontent citizens for assistance, arranged a plot to murder their masters and the colonial officers, and then to take upon themselves the government of the province.

The evening of the 13th of September was designated for the massacre; but upon the night of the 12th, a man by the name of Birkenhead, who was servant to a Mr. Smith of Purton, in Gloucester county, betrayed his accomplices.

Tidings of the discovery were immediately sent to Governor Berkeley, who ordered a party of militia to proceed at once to Poplar Spring, near Purton, which was the appointed rendezvous of the conspirators, and having secreted themselves to seize the miscreants as they came singly up. This scheme was successful only in part; a few of the earlier comers were taken prisoners, but others, making their escape, informed those who were behind, and the full extent of the conspiracy never becoming perfectly known, was doubtless much magnified.

For a time, the alarm growing out of the discovery of this plot was very great in Virginia. The assembly appointed a thanksgiving to be observed annually on the 13th of September. A guard was ordered for the protection of the governor and council, and a fort built at Jamestown, upon which several small pieces of cannon were mounted.

By an act of the English Parliament which went into operation during this year, all foreign goods intended for the colonies must first be landed in England, and be sent thence in English vessels. Under this act the English merchant obtained the entire control of the tobacco raised in Virginia; which, for want of any competition, he could purchase at his own valuation, while the Virginians were compelled to take such European goods as they required, in exchange, at any price the merchant might choose to ask.

To remedy this, the assembly endeavoured to raise the price of tobacco, by omitting to plant it for a year or more. But in order to render the scheme effectual, it was necessary to obtain the consent of Maryland to a similar restriction.

After much negotiation, the latter province, in

1666, passed an act ordering no tobacco to be planted for one year; but Lord Baltimore would not consent to its going into operation. Several other attempts were made to carry out a similar treaty, both with Maryland and the new province of Carolina, but they all proved abortive in the end.

The first exploring party that ever crossed the Blue Ridge was sent out from Virginia, by Berkeley, during this year. It consisted of fourteen Virginians, and as many Indians, the whole detachment being placed under the command of Captain Batt.

The party set out from Appomattox, and after a march of seven days reached the foot of the mountains. Those they first approached were neither high nor steep, but after they passed the first ridge, they encountered others which were so perpendicular, and so full of precipices, that it was with great difficutly they could travel three miles in a direct line in a whole day's march. In other places they found large level plains, dotted with groups of trees, and abounding with the deer, the elk, and the buffalo, so tame and gentle that they showed no fear at the appearance of the men, but would suffer them to approach within a few feet of them before they would change their quarters. After crossing other mountains, the exploring party came to a fine river, the stream of which they followed several days, until they came to old fields and cabins where the Indians had lately been. Batt left some toys in the deserted cabins, as an evidence of friendly feeling, and was about to continue his journey when his Indian allies refused to venture any farther.

They said, that not far off from that place, was a tribe of Indians which made salt, and sold it to the neighbouring savages; that this tribe was numerous and powerful, and never suffered any strangers to return after they had once entered their towns.

Finding the Indians resolute in their determination not to incur any more risk by prolonging the adventure, Captain Batt was compelled to return to the province, with all his high-wrought hopes of discovery frustrated.

The report of Batt to Governor Berkeley stimulated the latter to attempt the journey in person, but his preparations were defeated by growing difficulties within the province.

Notwithstanding the loyalty of the Virginians, the restoration of Charles II. had proved fatal to many of their most cherished rights and privileges. The authority of the crown was recognised in the choice of the governor and council; the justices of peace, who exercised the power of levying county taxes, received their appointment directly from the governor; the burgesses, previously elected every two years by universal suffrage, legislated themselves into an indefinite continuance of power; and finally, in 1670, although the system of direct taxation bore upon all freemen with a like equality, the assembly restricted the right of a voice in the election of burgesses to such only as were housekeepers and freeholders.

In 1671, the entire population of Virginia was estimated at forty thousand persons. Of this number, two thousand were negro slaves, and six thousand white indented apprentices. Of the latter, some fifteen hundred, mostly English, were imported annually. Of tobacco, the staple commodity, the quantity exported during the previous year was between fifteen and twenty thousand hogsheads, weighing three hundred and fifty pounds each. The ships trading to the province numbered some eighty. The executive consisted of the governor and fifteen councillors, subordinate to the assembly; the latter having full authority to levy such taxes as the exigencies of the province required. "We have forty-eight parishes," adds Berkeley, from whose letter to the privy council in England this account is taken, "and our ministers are well paid, and by my consent should be better, if they would pray oftener, and preach less." A little farther on, he thanks God there are neither schools nor printing-offices in the province, and hopes there will be none for a hundred years to come.

The poorer freemen of the province bore up under their various grievances and restrictions for several years, but with a gradually increasing impatience. The price of tobacco was extremely low, while the cost of foreign commodities had been enhanced; the taxes, bearing upon rich and poor alike, were oppressively unequal; while the franchise, a right which they had cherished so long, had become limited in its operation. The high wages which the burgesses had voted themselves, together with the cost of maintaining forts which were of little or no service, were also prolific sources of complaint. But all these evils of local origin were as nothing compared to the alarm into which the province was thrown by the magnificent vagaries of Charles II., its beloved sovereign.

His first freak was to give to one Colonel Norwood, for a term of years, the royal quitrents, instead of applying them to the benefit of the colony. His next, to grant to the Earl of St. Albans, Lord Culpepper, and others, the whole northern neck of Virginia; that is, the peninsula between the Rappahanock and the Potomac Rivers, without even excepting the plantations already settled there.

Finally, in 1673, the whole province was assigned, for thirty-one years, to Lords Culpepper and Arlington, including all quitrents, escheats, the power to grant lands, and to erect new counties; the presentation to new churches, and the nomination of sheriffs, escheators, and surveyors.

The nature of this assignment did not become known in the province until the following year. It was no sooner understood, however, than the whole people resolved to remonstrate. The assembly met, and after drawing up an address to his majesty, complaining of the grant as derogatory to previous charters and privileges, despatched three agents to England to solicit a modification of the grant, or to purchase it up for the benefit of the province.

To defray the charge of these agents, the assembly imposed upon the colonists—besides the ordinary taxes—a tax of one hundred pounds of tobacco per head, to be collected in two annual instalments, and amerced every unsuccessful suitor in the provincial courts, in a fine, ranging from thirty to seventy pounds of tobacco.

These taxes and amercements fell heaviest upon the poorer class of people, the profits of whose labour had scarcely been sufficient, in ordinary times, to feed and clothe their families. In 1674, the public dissatisfaction had broken out into popular disturbances, which were, however, speedily suppressed by a proclamation of the governor, aided by the calmer counsels of influential persons. But although quiet was thus restored, it was only for a brief season. Mere words were not sufficient to relieve positive suffering, and the people felt that their hardships still continued. Nor were many of the wealthier colonists insensible of the political change which the province had of late years undergone. They too looked back regretfully to former days of freedom and prosperity, and were ready to seize on any occasion which should offer them a favourable opportunity of asserting their ancient privileges. Time soon brought the occasion, and, with it, a leader around whom all classes of freemen could rally in a common cause.

During the year 1674, the Seneca Indians left their northern hunting-grounds, and precipitating themselves upon the Susquehannas, forced the latter to fall back on the borders of Maryland and Virginia. Several murders occurring in 1675, within the limits of Virginia, were retaliated upon the savages by the militia of the frontiers. War was declared, and as Maryland was at the time most seriously threatened, she received aid from the Virginia planters residing in the vicinity of the Potomac and Rappahannock Rivers.

These planters were commanded by John Washington, the great-grandfather of George Washington, a farmer settled in Westmoreland county, who had immigrated from England to Virginia some eighteen years before.

Having formed a junction with the Marylanders, the united forces attacked a fort of the Susquehannas on the north side of the Potomac, and—provoked, perhaps, by previous outrages—slew, in the heat of passion, six Indian chiefs who were sent out by the besieged to treat of peace. It was a treacherous act, and met with deserved reprobation. The leader of the Maryland militia was arrested by order of both houses of assembly, and narrowly escaped with his life; while Berkeley indignantly declared, "If they had killed my father and my mother, and all my friends, yet if they had come to treat of peace, they ought to have gone in peace."

After a desperate resistance the fort was taken, but the savages that escaped revenged the deaths of their slaughtered messengers by sacrificing ten colonists to each chief thus wantonly slain.

When this sanguinary retaliation was accomplished, they once more offered to treat for peace. But the passions of the Virginians were now fully aroused, and peace was refused. Berkeley himself, holding the monopoly of the beaver trade in Virginia, was inclined to favour the Indians. He was charged with being influenced more by his avarice than the safety of the province.

At this juncture, the tributary Indians, who had faithfully observed their treaty stipulations for thirty years, commenced a series of outrages upon the settlers. The people clamoured loudly for permission to defend themselves, and fixed upon Nathaniel Bacon for their leader.

Bacon was a young and wealthy planter,

scarcely thirty years of age, gifted with fine talents and an eloquent address. He had been educated in England, where he studied law in the Temple. On his return to Virginia he was called to a seat in the council, but being popularly inclined was no favourite with Berkeley, whose royalist and arbitrary tendencies gained strength with his advancing age. But the liberal opinions which lost Bacon the good graces of the governor gained him numerous friends among the people, who already began to look upon him as the champion of their cause. Dissensions arose in the council, and the vacillating conduct of the government at this juncture threw upon it the contempt of all who believed that the safety of the province required prompt and decisive action.

Bacon, after sending in vain to Jamestown for authority to organize an expedition against the Indians, asserted openly, that if another white man was murdered, he would take upon himself the authority which the people were desirous to confer, but which the government would neither grant nor refuse. Tidings were soon brought that some of Bacon's own men had been killed by the Indians on his plantation near the falls of the James River. Five hundred Virginians immediately flew to arms, and without waiting any longer for authority from Jamestown, Bacon placed himself at their head, and commenced his march against the enemy.

CHAPTER XV.

Departure of Bacon—Berkeley commands him to return and disperse his followers—Bacon attacks an Indian fort and carries it by storm—Is pursued by Berkeley—Disturbances in the lower counties—Dissolution of the old assembly—A new assembly called—Bacon elected a burgess—Is arrested by order of the governor—Temporary reconciliation—Bacon appointed commander-in-chief—Jealousy of Berkeley—Refuses Bacon a commission—Five hundred men march into Jamestown—Berkeley submits—Retires to Gloucester county—Proclaims Bacon a rebel—Bacon issues writs for a convention of the people—Berkeley retreats to Accomac—Raises an army and sails for Jamestown—Bacon marches against him—The governor deserted by his troops—Triumphant progress of Bacon—His death—Violent proceedings of Berkeley—Thomas Hansford and others hanged—Death of Berkeley.

The departure of Bacon was quickly made known to Berkeley. Irritated at finding his authority treated with contempt, the old governor issued a proclamation depriving Bacon of his seat in council, and commanding his followers to return to their homes. Such as feared the forfeiture of their estates obeyed, and Bacon was left to continue his march with only fifty-seven men. After penetrating the wilderness until his provisions were nearly exhausted, Bacon reached the vicinity of a fort of friendly Indians, from whom he offered to purchase such stores as the half famished condition of his men most imperatively required. The Indians readily promised to supply his wants, but for three days afterward delayed to fulfil their agreement. His food being entirely exhausted, and suspecting the garrison to be acting under secret advice from the governor, Bacon placed himself at the head of his followers, waded the deep stream flowing in front of the fort, and entreating the savages to furnish his men with food, tendered, at the same time, full payment for all that should be brought him.

While he was thus earnestly negotiating, a shot from the bank he had just quitted killed one of his men. His resolution was instantly taken. Fearful of an attack in the rear, he fired the palisades, stormed and burnt the fort and cabins, and with the loss of only three men, slew one hundred and fifty Indians.

In the mean time, Berkeley, instigated to extreme measures by the aristocratic faction in the province, levied troops and marched in pursuit of Bacon, but was soon compelled to retrace his steps.

To relieve their friend from the danger with which he was threatened, Drummond and Lawrence, both gentlemen of liberal principles, and of the highest standing in the community, fomented an insurrection in the lower counties. The people met by beat of drum, declared forts an intolerable nuisance, and giving vent to their long-pent-up hatred of the imperious assembly, demanded its dissolution. Berkeley, unable to contend against the popular voice, was compelled to submit. The assembly was dissolved; writs for a new election were issued; and Bacon, returning in triumph from his brief Indian campaign, was unanimously elected a burgess from his own county of Henrico.

Conscious of the danger he was likely to incur by proceeding to Jamestown alone, Bacon descended the river in a sloop, accompanied by forty armed followers. Thus protected, he waited on the governor and council for the purpose of justifying the course he had pursued. Being refused a hearing, he indignantly returned to his sloop and set sail for Henrico.

A longboat, filled with men, was immediately despatched to intercept him. Shots being fired, he exchanged the sloop for a small skiff, and retreated with greater speed up the river. Berkeley, however, had sent swift messengers, overland, to the ships lying at Sandy Point; and Bacon, finding his retreat cut off, surrendered to the summons of the sheriff, and with twenty of his followers was conveyed a prisoner to Jamestown.

But though the popular and patriotic young leader was now placed completely in his power, Berkeley did not dare to punish him with severity. The new assembly, which met in June, 1676, contained many burgesses who had espoused the liberal views of Bacon, and were diligently bent upon restoring those rights and privileges of which they had been deprived for several years.

The passionate old governor was induced to concede a pardon to the insurgents; while Bacon, moved thereto, perhaps, by the entreaties of his uncle—whose next heir he was—humbled himself before the assembly, and asked forgiveness of the past on the promise of future obedience.

By this means, and by the intervention of friends, a temporary reconciliation was effected with Berkeley, and Bacon was restored to his seat in council. The assembly appointed him soon after commander-in-chief, and the governor consented to sign his commission. The people were greatly rejoiced. It looked like the dawn of a happier day. The darling of their hopes had but stooped to conquer. The principles of Bacon rapidly gained ground, and many acts were passed by which much of the ancient freedom was restored.

Berkeley regarded these doings with a jealous eye. The particular pains taken by the assembly to redress old grievances was by no means palatable to him.

The activity of Lawrence and Drummond, both members of the assembly, was particularly obnoxious. He characterized them openly as rogues, and bade the burgesses beware of them; bade them despatch the Indian business, and meddle with nothing else till that was done. The increasing popularity of Bacon, his eloquence, his engaging manners, his blameless life, and, above all, his freely expressed sentiments of patriotism, kept the suspicions of the governor constantly on the alert. When liberal principles wholly prevailed in Virginia, Berkeley had acknowledged himself the servant of the burgesses. The royalist tendencies of the latter, and a grasping desire on their part to maintain their seats for life, had led them to contract the liberties of the people, and to surrender to the crown the appointment of the governor and council, in the hope of retaining for themselves a permanence of office. With increase of power, Berkeley grew imperious and dogmatic. He was no longer the servant of the assembly, but its arrogant master, and any attempt to resist his dictation, or to infringe upon what he considered his prerogative, was, in his opinion, a crime little short of treason to the crown.

Bacon, from his commanding talents, and the affection with which he was regarded by the masses, soon became to Berkeley an object of fear and dislike, and the impetuous old man was but a poor dissembler. When, therefore, Berkeley was requested to sign the commission of Bacon as commander-in-chief, he refused. Bacon immediately left Jamestown, and in a few days re-entered it at the head of five hundred men.

These sturdy followers, after surrounding the statehouse while the burgesses were in session, clamoured loudly for a commission to their leader, and indemnity for their present act.

Presenting their fusils at the windows of the apartment where the burgesses met, and which was then crowded with faces, they repeated the demand for the commission, adding menacingly, "We'll have it! we'll have it!" One of the members then waved his handkerchief to them from the window, and cried out, "You shall have it, you shall have it!" Upon this promise the men unbent their locks, and grounding their arms waited till Bacon should rejoin them.

No sooner was the presence of the latter at the head of an armed force known to Berkeley, than, accompanied by his council, he went out to meet him. There was no want of courage in the testy old governor. Baring his breast as he advanced, he cried out to Bacon, "A fair mark! shoot!" The reply of the young leader was calm. "No, may it please your honour," said he, "we will not hurt a hair of your head, nor of any other man's. We are come for a commission to save our lives from the Indians, which you have so often promised; and now we'll have it before we go." On the second day, Berkeley, pressed on all sides, was compelled to submit. A commission was issued, appointing Bacon general of all the forces then raising in Virginia, and a despatch was transmitted to England, signed by the governor, his council, and the burgesses, commending the legislation of the new assembly, and the zeal, loyalty, and patriotism of Bacon.

Energetic operations were at once commenced against the savages. As preliminary to the campaign for which the troops were organizing, the thickets and swamps were pierced by scouting parties of rangers, and the stragglers of the enemy driven back upon the main body.

At length, when Bacon was prepared to put his little army in motion, Berkeley retired to Gloucester county, called a convention of the inhabitants, and against the openly avowed opinions of those whom he had summoned together, proclaimed Bacon a rebel.

Berkeley's "two rogues," Lawrence and Drummond—the former an Oxford scholar, and the latter but recently governor of the new province of North Carolina—immediately bore the tidings to Bacon in his camp. Conscious of being inspired by none other than patriotic motives, Bacon appealed at once from the irascible governor to the people of Virginia, whom he called upon, by all they held most dear, to meet in convention and shake off the tyranny of Berkeley.

His summons was responded to with alacrity. The ablest and best men in the province assembled at Middle Plantation—now Williamsburg. Many excellent speeches were made, but those of Bacon were superior to any. The whole convention promised, under the sanctity of an oath, to support him in the war against the Indians, and to make common cause with him, even against troops from England, until such time as a correct statement of affairs could be laid before the king.

Berkeley now retreated across the bay to Accomac county, accompanied by Beverly, Ludwell, and a few other ultra loyalist partisans. Here he succeeded in collecting, by profuse promises of pay and plunder, a force of nearly one thousand men. With this army, in two ships and sixteen sloops, he sailed up the James River, and on the 8th of September, 1676, encamped at Jamestown.

In the mean time, Bacon had not been idle. Acting upon the advice of Drummond, Lawrence, and other patriotic counsellors, the retreat of Berkeley to the eastern shore was proclaimed an abdication of his government, and writs were issued by Bacon and four of his colleagues, calling upon the people to send delegates to a new convention.

No act could have been more popular with the great majority of the people. Even the women of the province expressed their joy on this occasion. Sarah Drummond, the wife of the patriotic ex-governor of North Carolina, said, "The child that is unborn shall have cause to rejoice for the good that will come by the rising of the country."

"If we overcome the governor, a greater power from England will ruin us in return," said Ralph Weldinge. Sarah Drummond smiled contemptuously. Taking from the ground a small stick, she broke it in two pieces as she replied, "I fear no more the power of England than a broken straw."

Always resolute and cheerful, this noble hearted woman animated the troops with a portion of her own enthusiasm; and in the midst of increasing dangers, cried out hopefully, "We shall do well enough."

As soon as tidings were received that Berkeley again occupied Jamestown, and in force, swift messengers were despatched throughout the province, calling upon the planters to arm in defence of their liberties. Drummond and Lawrence immediately set out to join Bacon, who had just disbanded his troops after a successful expedition against the Pamunkey Indians.

A new force was speedily collected, and though it was still inferior to that under Berkeley, Bacon determined to march at once upon Jamestown.

In order to enable him to throw up his intrenchments without annoyance from the loyalists, Bacon despatched small parties of horse to bring in from the neighbouring plantations the wives of such gentlemen as had taken up arms in support of the governor. These he displayed on the crest of his unfinished works; but when the latter were completed, the ladies were removed beyond the reach of harm. Berkeley, confident in his numbers, sallied out at once to attack the patriots; but being repulsed with loss, his followers deserted him in search of plunder, and the old governor was compelled to embark hastily on board his ships during the night, and retreat down the river to Accomac.

The following morning Bacon entered Jamestown. To prevent it from becoming a second time a place of refuge for the loyalists, it was determined in a council of war to lay the town in ashes. Drummond and Lawrence, the owners of the best houses in the place, set the example, by each putting fire to his own dwelling.

Jamestown being destroyed, even to the church, the first that ever was in Virginia, Bacon marched against Colonel Brent, who was advancing from Accomac at the head of a reinforcement of twelve hundred men. On the approach of the little army of patriots, Brent was deserted by his troops, and hastily fell back from whence he came; while Bacon, having revolutionized with ease the entire western shore, made his preparations to cross the bay, and subject the only small strip of territory which yet acknowledged the authority of Berkeley.

But the malaria of the marshes around Jamestown was more fatal to the cause of the young patriot general than the arms of the aristocratic Cavaliers. He was attacked by a malignant fever caught by sleeping in the trenches, and on the 1st of October he died.

With the loss of Bacon ended the hopes of the patriots. The new leader, Ingram, did not possess either the talent or the popularity of his former chief. Berkeley exerted himself with renewed activity; and having entire possession of the naval force of the province, was soon enabled to attack separate detachments of the patriots, and beat them in detail.

Thomas Hansford, a native of the colony, was the first partisan officer that was taken prisoner. Young, gay, reckless, with a keen sense of honour, and a sincere love for his country, his fate was regarded with the greatest commiseration. After his sentence had been announced to him, he asked no favour of the governor but that he "might be shot like a soldier, and not hanged like a dog." Berkeley replied vindictively, "You die not as a soldier, but as a rebel!"

Turning to the assembled crowd, as he approached the gibbet, Hansford said: "Take notice, I die a loyal subject, and a lover of my country."

Two other partisan leaders, Cheeseman and Wilford, were captured shortly after, upon the

York River. Wilton was the son of a royalist knight, who had died fighting for Charles I. Alluding to the eye which he had lost in the late skirmish, he said jocosely, "If I was stark blind, the governor would afford me a guide to the gallows."

"Why did you engage in Bacon's designs?" demanded Berkeley, at the trial of Cheeseman.

"My provocations," said his wife, stepping forward, "made my husband join in the cause for which Bacon contended; but for me he had never done what he has done." Then falling on her knees, she continued: "Since what is done was done by my means, I am most guilty; let me be hanged, but let my husband be pardoned."

"Away!" exclaimed Berkeley, adding, in the fierceness of his passion, a term of reproach that sullied the lips which uttered it.

When Drummond was brought in a prisoner, Berkeley made him a profound bow. "You are very welcome," said he; "I am more glad to see you than any man in Virginia; you shall be hanged in half an hour." In three hours he was dead.

Berkeley's thirst for blood increased with the means of gratification. Twenty-two persons were hanged in spite of remonstrances and intercessions.

"The old fool," said Charles II., "has taken

away more lives in that naked country, than I for the murder of my father."

The commissioners who had been sent over by the king to inquire into the origin of the disturbances censured the conduct of Berkeley. The English people expressed in loud terms their detestation of his sanguinary measures; and Berkeley, who had returned to England with the vessel which had borne the commissioners to Virginia, took the public reprobation so much to heart, that he sickened and died almost immediately after his arrival in London.

CHAPTER XVI.

Jeffreys appointed governor—An attempt made to regulate the Indian traffic—Political restrictions again enforced—Chicheley deputy-governor—Arrival of Lord Culpepper—Appointed governor for life—His avaricious disposition—Defrauds the troops—Returns to England—Administration of Chicheley—Impoverished condition of the province—Discontent of the people—Return of Culpepper to Virginia—Compromises with the planters of the northern neck—Embarks for England—Lord Howard appointed governor—His meanness and avarice—Transportation of prisoners for political offences—Their reception in Virginia—Administration of Nicholson—Project for a college—A charter obtained—Andros appointed governor—His neatness and method—Is succeeded by Nicholson.

Upon Berkeley's embarkation for England, Herbert Jeffreys was appointed governor. He made soon after a treaty of peace with the Indians. In October, 1677, a new assembly was convened, which attempted to regulate the future traffic with the Indians, by limiting it to certain fixed places, at which the traders and the savages were to meet semi-annually.

But these regulations were soon violated by the Indians, who conceived that the treaty of peace remained imperfect while they were restricted in their mode of dealing. After an ineffectual attempt to systematize the traffic according to the law, the rules were abandoned as impracticable.

The death of Bacon was peculiarly unfortunate for Virginia in many respects. The liberal opinions he had encouraged and sustained found no open advocacy after the terrible punishment awarded by Berkeley to the prominent prisoners who had fallen into his hands. The right to define the form of government was taken from the people, and assumed by the crown. The assemblies were thenceforth to be called only once in two years, and the session was limited to fourteen days. The old restriction upon the franchise was restored under an order from the king, which directed that freeholders alone should be entitled to elect the members of assembly. All the old grievances returned, many of them in an aggravated shape, and the aristocratic faction were once more in full possession of their former supremacy.

On the death of Jeffreys, which took place in December, 1678, Sir Henry Chicheley, who had been deputy-governor under Berkeley, produced his old commission, and his authority was acknowledged by the council until a new governor should arrive from England.

In April, 1679, the assembly met at Middle Plantation, and ordered forts to be built and garrisoned on the Rappahannock, the Matapony, the Potomac, and James Rivers.

In the spring of 1680, Lord Culpepper arrived in Virginia. He had obtained from the facile Charles, besides the immense tract of land lying between the Potomac and the Rappahannock, an appointment as governor of Virginia for life. An assembly was convened in June, and three acts, already passed and ratified in England, were offered to the burgesses for their acceptance. The first, and most grateful to their feelings, was an act granting general pardon and oblivion for all transgressions and outrages committed in the time of Bacon's rebellion. The second, took the power to naturalize foreigners out of the hands of the assembly and placed it in those of the governor. The third, of a far more grievous character, was also accepted, though not without encountering severe opposition, for it authorized a perpetual export duty of two shillings on every hogshead of tobacco, and granted the proceeds as a royal revenue for the support of the government, to be accounted for, not to the assembly, but to the king.

Lord Culpepper was less evil disposed, politically, toward the colonists, than avaricious to make the most he could out of them in the shortest possible space of time.

In consideration of his being a peer, he obtained of the king a salary of two thousand a year as governor of Virginia, instead of one thousand as previously allowed. He also received one hundred and fifty pounds a year for house rent, in addition to the usual perquisites.

The latter, Culpepper took especial pains to increase in every possible way. It had been customary previously, for all masters of vessels trading to Virginia, to make certain presents of liquors and provisions toward the governor's housekeeping. These presents Culpepper remitted, and received instead, as a duty, twenty shillings on every vessel of less than a hundred tons, and thirty shillings for all over that burthen. The amount being ordered to be paid regularly at each clearance of the ship.

Culpepper had other schemes also for raising money. The standard of value being higher in the neighbouring colonies than in Virginia, he proposed to the assembly to raise it to an equality with others. The assembly consented, and were about to pass a law for that purpose, when his lordship stopped them, and told them as it was a part of the king's prerogative, it would be better for himself as governor to effect the change by proclamation.

The money for the payment of the regiment of soldiers sent over during Bacon's rebellion passing through Culpepper's hands, he had bought up, at a reduced price, light pieces of eight—a silver coin approximating in value to the modern dollar. He now issued a proclamation for raising the value of pieces of eight from five to six shillings. As soon as the coin passed current at the new rate, he produced an order for the payment and disbanding of the troops; but when his own salary and perquisites were about to be paid in coin at the same high estimate, Culpepper again made use of his prerogative to reduce the value of money to its former standard.

In less than a year he returned to England, leaving Sir Henry Chicheley deputy-governor. The rapacity of Culpepper, and the pursuance of a similar system of extortion by Chicheley, so impoverished the province, that the planters were only restrained with great difficulty from breaking out into open revolt. Had not the disastrous issue of Bacon's rebellion, and the sanguinary excesses committed afterward, taught them the prudence of curbing their resentment, there is no doubt that a serious insurrection would have arisen out of the oppressed condition of the province. As it was, disturbances were continually occurring, which kept Chicheley and his council in constant alarm. These were not wholly quieted until Culpepper again reached Virginia in 1682, and hanged, in a summary manner, a few of the most prominent offenders.

The design of Culpepper in returning to a country which was distasteful to him as a place of residence, was for the purpose of reviving his claim to the northern neck. In this object he was so far successful as to compel the planters to negotiate a compromise.

In May, 1683, he again embarked for England; and the council, soon after, taking into consideration the impoverished condition of Virginia, petitioned the king to recall his grant to Arlington and Culpepper.

The petition was successful. Arlington surrendered his rights; the patent to Culpepper was annulled by process of law; and, in July 1684, Virginia again became a royal province, of which Lord Howard of Effingham was appointed governor.

The new governor was soon found to be as avaricious of money as his predecessors. He required a license to be taken out by all schoolmasters and members of the bar. He extorted excessive fees for putting the official seal to probates of wills and letters of administration, even where the estates of the deceased were of the meanest value. He even descended so low as to share the perquisites of office with his clerks.

In 1685, James II. ascended the English throne. The rebellion of the Duke of Monmouth, a natural son of the late king, took place soon after. When the bloody executions which followed its suppression were in a measure checked, many of the unfortunate prisoners who had escaped with their lives, were condemned to be transported to the colonies, for terms of years never less than ten, where they were sold to the planters as servants.

The demand for labour was at this time so great in the plantations, that the convicts and labourers shipped from abroad were purchased at from ten to fifteen pounds each. Of those transported by the sanguinary Jeffreys for their participation in Monmouth's rebellion, many were gentlemen by birth and education. Against such, James was excessively severe. Under the countersign of his minister Sunderland, he wrote to the governor and council of Virginia: "Take all care that they shall serve for ten years at least; and that they be not permitted to redeem themselves, by money or otherwise, until that term be fully expired. Prepare a bill for the assembly of our colony, with such clauses as shall be requisite for this purpose."

But the Virginia assembly were not inclined to follow the dictation of the king. No bill was passed. The exiles were received in the province with that commiseration which their misfortunes merited. Immediately after the accession of William and Mary, in 1689, all those who had been transported to the colonies for political offences received a full pardon.

After the downfall of James II., Lord Howard of Effingham returned to England, leaving the duties of governor to Colonel Nathaniel Bacon. The administration of Bacon was brief, and unmarked by any occurrence worthy of notice. In 1690, Francis Nicholson, who had been appointed lieutenant-governor under Howard, reached Virginia and immediately assumed the duties of his office.

The business of Nicholson was to recommend himself to the people of Virginia, and through them to the new government in England. He accordingly sought to ingratiate himself by patronizing sports and games of various kinds, and by awarding prizes to all who excelled in the exercises of riding, running, shooting, wrestling, and backsword. A project for a college, which had been for some time in agitation, was warmly encouraged by the new governor. He declined, nevertheless, to call an assembly for the purpose of taking the matter into consideration, but acceded to a proposition for a general subscription, to which he personally contributed largely. His example was promptly followed. Aided by the generous contributions of several merchants in London, the sum raised within the year, amounted to two thousand five hundred pounds.

When the assembly was convened in 1691, it entered heartily into the proposed scheme for a college. An address in its favour was drawn up and transmitted to England, and the Reverend Mr. Blair sent out to obtain from the joint sovereigns, William and Mary, a charter for the same. The envoy was peculiarly successful in his mission. He obtained a charter such as the people of the province desired. Their majesties also gave, toward the founding of the college, the balance due on account of quitrents, amounting to nearly two thousand pounds sterling; while toward its endowment, they allowed twenty thousand acres of choice land, together with the revenue arising from tobacco exported from Virginia and Maryland to the other plantations.

In 1692, Nicholson was succeeded as governor-in-chief by Sir Edmund Andros. During the six years the latter remained in office, many reforms were introduced by him from which the colony received considerable benefit. Andros was one of the most methodical of men, and through his nice sense of neatness and order, the office of the provincial secretary underwent an entire revision. Important documents had hitherto been thrust negligently into the first vacant space that offered. Many original patents, records, and deeds, with other papers of importance, had been scattered loosely about the office until they were partly eaten by the moths, or otherwise soiled and mutilated. These irregularities were speedily reformed. The governor caused the loose and torn records of value to be transcribed into new books, and ordered shelves and closets to be constructed for their better preservation in future. He had scarcely ceased to congratulate himself upon the completion of his labours, when the State House took fire in the month of October, 1698, and was burned to the ground. Notwithstanding this calamity, and in despite of the brief period yet remaining before his term of office expired, the governor caused all the records and papers saved from the fire to be properly arranged and registered, and in this excellent condition turned them over to Nicholson, who had been appointed his successor.

CHAPTER XVII.

Administration of Nicholson—Williamsburg founded—Dissenters tolerated by statute—Enormous power of the governor—Modes of its restriction—Bold project of De Callier, Governor of Montreal—How defeated—English scheme of general defence for the colonies—Virginia refuses her quota—Nicholson's letter in consequence—Loses his popularity—Political discontent—Nicholson removed—The office of Governor of Virginia granted as a sinecure to the Earl of Orkney—Edward Nott appointed deputy governor—Revised code of Virginia—Prominent provisions—Jennings president of the council — Succeeds Nott — Colonel Spotswood appointed deputy-governor—Crosses the Blue Ridge—Is knighted—Is succeeded by Hugh Drysdale—Death of Drysdale—Accession of Brigadier-general Gooch.

THE administration of Nicholson, though extending from 1698 to 1705, was comparatively quiet and uneventful. The first object to which he turned his attention, was to obtain from the assembly the passage of an act to build a new city which should constitute in future the capital of the province, instead of the unfortunate and insalubrious Jamestown.

Middle Plantation, where the new college buildings had already been erected, had been found by constant experience to be healthy and agreeable to the constitutions of the inhabitants of the colony, having the natural advantages of a serene and temperate air, and a fine open country, well watered with springs. It likewise possessed the additional convenience of two navigable creeks running out of James and York rivers. Two hundred and twenty acres of the tract were accordingly purchased for the use of the colony, and laid out in half-acre lots. The streets of the new city, in evidence of the loyalty of the colonists, were arranged in the form of a cipher, made of the letters W and M, in honour of William and Mary, and the name given to the future capital was Williamsburg.

As a means of defraying the expenses of building the State House, the tax previously placed on liquor, and a new tax on servants and slaves—not English—imported into the colony, were appropriated to that purpose.

During the same session, a resolution was passed for a complete revisal of the colonial laws. In obedience to orders from England, the assembly also granted, by statute, the benefit of the English toleration acts to dissenters. This was the beginning of religious freedom in Virginia.

But if the commands of the crown constrained the Virginians to recognise the rights of nonconformists, the ancient political privileges of the province were still withheld. From the period of Bacon's rebellion the power of the governor had increased. "He was lieutenant-general and admiral, lord treasurer and chancellor, the chief judge in all courts, president of the council, and bishop, or ordinary; so that the armed force, the revenue, the interpretation of law, the administration of justice, the church—all were under his control or guardianship."

Three restrictions upon the abuse of this authority existed, in the instructions from abroad, in the council, and in the vote of the general assembly; but as the instructions were not divulged, as the council were dependent upon the chief magistrate for their seats and prospective advancement, and as the assembly not only occupied a subordinate position, but lay under the constant surveillance of the clerk—who held his office from the governor—had the latter been disposed to tyrannize, few would have been found bold enough to censure his acts.

Great, however, as the power of the governor really was, it was seldom exercised to the injury of the people. The latter had, indeed, by assenting to the establishment of a perpetual revenue, crippled their means of resistance, but, as the governor was often compelled to call upon the burgesses for additional supplies, they claimed the right of appointing a treasurer subject to themselves only, and when this privilege was denied them by the crown, Virginia declined to contribute its quota to the defence of the colonies against France.

Previous to 1692, the French governor of Montreal, the Count De Callier, viewing with alarm the rapid growth of the English colonies, formed the daring project of separating the eastern provinces from those of the south, by the capture of New York. This plan having been adopted by the French government, a fleet was sent, in September, 1692, to take possession of the bay of New York, with orders to co-operate with a land force which was to have marched from Quebec by way of the Sorel river and Lake Champlain.

This bold and well planned scheme, was however, rendered abortive by a sudden invasion of Canada. The fierce and warlike tribes constituting the five nations, suddenly spread terror and desolation throughout the French possessions, and compelled the governor to employ the force destined to operate upon New York, in guarding weak points at home, or in waging ineffectual battle against the wary and sanguinary savages.

To prevent the project of De Callier from being carried into effect at some future day, the English government, in 1695, devised a plan of general defence, the charges of which were to be borne by the respective provinces according to the ratio of population.

To the great disappointment of Nicholson, with whom the plan was a favourite, and in direct opposition to orders from England, the Virginia assembly unanimously refused to appropriate any moneys for the purpose required, on the ground that "no forts then in being, nor any others that might be built in the province of New York, could in the least avail in the defence or security of Virginia, since either the French or the northern Indians might invade the colony, and not come within a hundred miles of such forts."

Nicholson himself took this refusal by no means placidly. He even wrote to the king, suggesting that Virginia should be coerced into acquiescence. The reply of William was but little suited to the bustling and ardent character of his governor. The monarch merely recommended that the matter should be again referred to the General Assembly.

This imprudent act on the part of their once popular governor, brought Nicholson into collision, both with his council and the assembly. Roused by the quarrel, the people were led to examine, somewhat narrowly, the manner in which they had lately been governed. They no sooner made the discovery that other provinces were in the enjoyment of greater privileges than themselves, than they grew dissatisfied, and demanded to be placed on an equal political footing with the most favoured of the colonies.

The difficulties of Governor Nicholson now rapidly increased. His conduct in many instances having been of a character that would not bear close scrutiny, the council, which was composed of the wealthiest men in the province, were at length able to make such representations as led to his removal in 1705.

The office of Governor of Virginia was no sooner declared vacant, than Anne, who had ascended the English throne, bestowed it as a sinecure for life upon the Earl of Orkney. Subsequently, during a period of nearly fifty years, the office was held in this manner; the nominal governor receiving three-fifths of the salary, or twelve hundred pounds sterling annually; the remaining two-fifths, or eight hundred pounds, being paid to a deputy-governor, by whom the duties were actually performed.

The first deputy-governor under the new arrangement was Edward Nott. During his brief administration, a new digest of the laws of Virginia, which had been in preparation for several years by a committee of the council and burgesses, was reported to the assembly, and passed.

Many of the provisions of this code relate to indented servants and slaves. All children were declared to be bond or free according to the condition of their mothers. Negroes, mulattoes, and Indians, were not allowed to purchase Christian servants. Servants not indentured, if over nineteen, were to serve for five years; if under nineteen, then until the age of twenty-four.

Every male servant completing his time of service, was entitled to receive, at his dismissal, ten bushels of Indian corn, thirty shillings in money or goods, and one well-fixed musket or fusee, of the value of twenty shillings at the least. Every woman servant, on acquiring her freedom, could claim fifteen bushels of Indian corn, and forty shillings in money, or goods.

Each county was allowed two burgesses, and Jamestown one, to be elected by the freeholders. All properly qualified persons neglecting to vote were liable to a penalty of two hundred pounds of tobacco. The travelling expenses of the burgesses were graduated and defined. Those coming by land, receiving one hundred and thirty pounds of tobacco per day; while such as came by water, received one hundred and twenty pounds.

The twelve members of the council were to receive three hundred and fifty pounds sterling, above sixteen hundred dollars, annually, to be proportioned among them according to the time of their attendance. Such were the most important provisions of the revised code of 1705.

Governor Nott survived his appointment only one year; in 1706 he died. The deputy-governorship was then given to Brigadier-general Hunter; but he being captured by the French on his passage out, Edmund Jennings, president of the council, continued for four years to perform the duties of the office.

In 1710, Colonel Alexander Spotswood, an officer of fine talents, urbane and conciliating in his manners, yet active and enterprising, arrived in Virginia, bearing the commission of deputy-governor.

He had been but a short time in the province before he organized an expedition to cross the Blue Ridge. This was successfully accomplished. Spotswood, gallantly attended by a troop of horse, passed the mountains, which from the time of Berkeley had presented a barrier to the advance of the whites, and discovered the fine valley lying beyond. Although this exploration did not lead to any immediate result of importance, the service performed by Spotswood was considered of sufficient consequence to entitle him to the honour of knighthood.

The thirteen years during which the latter held office as deputy-governor of Virginia, glided away in almost unruffled political tranquillity.

In 1711 he wrote of his government, as being "in perfect peace and tranquillity, under a due obedience to the royal authority, and a gentlemanly conformity to the Church of England." Notwithstanding this hearty eulogy, Spotswood, in the course of his official career, several times found that councils could be stubborn, and assemblies refractory. With one so desirous of promoting the best interests of the colony as the gallant deputy governor, the differences which occasionally arose between himself and his colleagues, were never either very important, or of long continuance. Explanations and concessions soon restored them to a mutually good understanding, and the machinery of government again worked easily and harmoniously.

In 1723, Spotswood was superseded in his office by Hugh Drysdale. During the four following years a general harmony and contentment prevailed throughout the province. In 1727 Drysdale died, sincerely lamented by the assembly as a just and disinterested man. He was succeeded by Brigadier-general Gooch, under whose prolonged administration, Virginia continued for many years to enjoy profound peace and uninterrupted prosperity.

CHAPTER XVIII.

The Eastern provinces—War of 1689—French territorial claims—Movements of Count Frontenac—Cocheco burned by Casteno—Pemaquid taken by the Penobscot Indians—Burning of Schenectady—Massacre at Salem Falls—Capture of the Casco Bay settlement—First American Congress—Unsuccessful attempt upon Quebec—Acadie invaded by Sir William Phipps—Expedition of Church—Villebon recaptures Port Royal—York destroyed by the French—Wells successfully defended—Virginia votes five hundred pounds towards the defence of New York—Frontenac ravages the territory of the Five Nations—Success of D'Ibberville—Church ravages the French settlements—Burning of Haverhill and Andover—Peace of Ryswick—Plan of co-operation foı the colonies—French construct a line of posts from Canada to Louisiana—Alarm of the English—Renewal of the war—French and Indian excesses—Surprise of Deerfield—Expedition against Acadie—Haverhill burned—Port Royal taken—Inglorious expedition of Sir Hoveden Walker.

But, while Virginia, with some restrictions upon her political freedom, had been for many years in the enjoyment of profound peace, the colonies to the eastward were, during the same period, the victims of several sanguinary episodes, originating from the revengeful character of the Northern Indians, and the jealousy of the Canadian French.

The European war of 1689, necessarily involved in a contest those colonies of France and England which were contiguous to each other. The French population of America was comparatively small, being less than twelve thousand; but the French claims upon the territory of the North American continent were large, and quite as just as claims founded upon discovery usually are. Over Canada, Hudson's Bay, and Newfoundland, the dominion of France had been successfully asserted; while from the heroic explorations of La Salle, Marquette, and numerous devoted missionaries, a claim had been set up to one-half of Maine and Vermont, to more than half of New York, to the whole valley of the Mississippi, and to Texas as far as the Rio Bravo del Norte. The claims of England rested upon the original discovery of the continent by the elder Cabot. The French were not in possession of any sea-coast or harbours, properly so called: but had confined their plantations to the banks of the two great rivers, the St. Lawrence and the Mississippi; the one running south, and the other nearly north, their sources being at no great distance from each other, and forming a line almost parallel to the sea-coast inhabited by the English. Up to this period very few of the latter had made settlements more than a hundred miles distant from the coast, although in point of numbers they were already, in comparison with the French, as twenty to one.

No sooner did the existence of war between France and England become known in Canada, than Count Frontenac prepared for that memorable attempt upon New York, which was so signally frustrated by a sudden irruption of the Iroquois Indians, an irruption which carried terror and desolation to the very gates of Montreal.

But if New York was thus unexpectedly saved from the horrors of invasion, the eastern provinces were less fortunate. The Penacook warriors, under the French leader Castine, fell suddenly upon the defenceless village of Cocheco, during the night of the twenty-seventh of June, 1689, killed three and twenty persons, burned several houses, and bore away through the wilderness twenty-nine captives. Incited by the Jesuit Thury, the Penobscot Indians, to the number of a hundred warriors, paddled silently towards Pemaquid, another frontier English settlement, murdered such labourers as were found in the fields, assaulted the stockade fort, and, after an obstinate defence of two days, compelled the garrison to surrender themselves prisoners of war.

In the midst of the winter of 1690, a party of one hundred and ten French and Indians marched from Montreal, waded through snows and morasses for twenty-two days, and entered just before midnight the unguarded village of Schenectady, a Dutch settlement on the Mohawk, set the houses on fire, and then roused the inhabitants from their slumbers with the shrill and fearful sound of the savage whoop. Sixty were massacred, of whom seventeen were children, and ten Africans.

Towards the close of March, another French war party, led by the inhuman Hertel, after crossing the mountains and threading the forests of New Hampshire, attacked by surprise the frontier village at Salmon Falls; killed most of the male inhabitants, and carried off as prisoners fifty-four persons, nearly all of whom were women and children. These were burdened with the spoils taken from their own homes. One aged man the savages burned on the way by a slow fire. Mary Ferguson, a girl of fifteen, was scalped because she wept from fatigue; and of two infants, one was dashed against a tree, and the other thrown into the river, that their wretched mothers, thus relieved of their precious burdens, might not delay the rapid movement of the victors.

While thus returning, laden with prisoners and spoils, Hertel met a third detachment sent out by Frontenac, and a junction of forces being agreed upon, they proceeded to attack the fort and settlement at Casco Bay. A part of the garrison was decoyed into an ambuscade, and cut off almost to a man. The remainder held out until their palisades were about to be fired, when they surrendered on terms as prisoners of war.

This new and terrible mode of warfare, wherein

Indian ferocity was guided by French skill and enterprise, admonished the English colonies of the necessity of joining together and making common cause against the French Canadians, and their barbarous allies.

Out of this necessity originated the first American Congress, which met at New York on the first day of May, 1690. Massachusetts had taken the initiative by addressing circular letters to all the colonies as far south as Maryland; inviting them to send commissioners to New York, to agree upon some concerted plan of operations. Delegates from Massachusetts, Connecticut, and New York met accordingly, and arrangements were entered into, by which, while Massachusetts despatched a fleet and army against Quebec by water, nine hundred men from Connecticut and New York were to march overland against Montreal. Owing to the indefatigable exertions of Count Frontenac, and the warlike alacrity of his savage allies, both these expeditions terminated disastrously. An enterprise previously undertaken by Massachusetts had met with better success. A fleet of nine small vessels, containing between seven and eight hundred men, had been sent against Acadie, now known as New Brunswick and Nova Scotia.

The command of this fleet was entrusted to Sir William Phipps, who has made his name famous in the history of America for his successful recovery of an immense treasure from a Spanish wreck, on the coast of St. Domingo. Phipps conquered with great ease the French settlements in Acadie, and brought away with him sufficient plunder to pay the whole expense of the expedition.

In the mean time, Colonel Church, a provincial officer of great ability, marched against the eastern Indians, destroyed their settlements on the Androscoggin, and, for the sake of example, put a number of his prisoners to death, not sparing even women or children.

The retaliation of the eastern tribes was immediate. A frontier warfare was kept up incessantly during the whole of 1691. Many of the towns in Maine were abandoned entirely, and all of them suffered more or less.

The French also were again in motion. Villebon, with one small vessel of war, retook Port Royal, where Phipps had left a garrison, and stimulated the fierce animosity of the eastern Indians by timely presents and frequent supplies of arms and ammunition. The village of York, in Maine, was suddenly attacked by a party of French and Indians, and suffered a loss of seventy-five in killed, and an equal number carried off prisoners to Canada. The town of Wells was more fortunate; the inhabitants being apprised in time of the coming danger, successfully encountered their enemies and beat them off with loss.

The extensive frontier of New York offering at all times great facilities to invasion from Canada, five companies of regular troops were sent from England, in 1694, to assist in its defence, and a definite quota of men and money required by the English government to be contributed by each province in case of urgent necessity. The Indian war still continuing, a council was held at Albany, in August 1694, with the chiefs of the Five Nations, for the purpose of securing the latter from the insidious influence of the French. Deputies from Massachusetts, Connecticut, New York, and New Jersey, were present at this council. In 1695, the assembly of Virginia reluctantly voted five hundred pounds sterling toward the defence of New York; but requested of the crown to be excused from making any further grants. The aversion of the middle and southern provinces to advance their quotas for the conduct of the war, caused it to languish on the part of the English, who thereby gave the energetic French governor an opportunity to ravage the territory of the Onondagos and Oneidas, always the faithful allies of the English, by which they were compelled to sue for peace.

D'Ibberville, who had previously distinguished himself by a descent upon the English settlements at Hudson's Bay, captured the Massachusetts fort at Pemaquid, and broke up entirely the plantations at that neighbourhood. He next proceeded to Newfoundland, where he took the fort of St. John's, and captured several inferior posts scattered over that Island. From thence he proceeded to Hudson's Bay, where he recaptured a fort previously taken by the English, and made prizes of two English vessels.

The veteran Church retaliated by leading an expedition against the French settlements on the bay of Fundy. He succeeded in driving the inhabitants from Beau Bassin, in burning their houses, and in destroying their cattle; but he failed in his attempt to recapture the fort of St. John's, Newfoundland.

Flushed with the successes of the French, their savage allies, during the winter of 1697, penetrated to within twenty-five miles of Boston, and made successful assaults upon the towns of Haverhill and Andover, murdering many of the inhabitants, and leading others prisoners into Canada.

The treaty of peace between England and France, which was signed at Ryswick, in September, 1697, at length put an end to the war that had so long desolated the colonial frontiers, while it gave to each nation, possession of all the places respectively held at the commencement of hostilities.

The terrible struggle through which the more exposed colonies had passed, naturally urged the adoption for the future of some system of co-operation by which all the colonies should contribute proportionately toward the common defence. The Board of Trade—which had recently been organized in London for the purpose of supervising colonial affairs—suggested the propriety of commissioning a captain-general for the colonies, who should receive his appointment from the king, and be vested with full powers to call out and command, the colonial militia. A counter-project, proposed by William Penn, though laid aside soon after, with the less popular plan of the Board of Trade, is peculiarly interesting as being in substance similar to the one adopted by the colonies, when, at a subsequent period, they determined to resist taxation by the English government. Penn proposed a Colonial Congress of twenty members, to be chosen annually by the assemblies, with a president to be named by the king, the Congress to be empowered during war to provide for the common defence, and in peace, to regulate commerce and adjust colonial disputes.

No sooner was the peace of Ryswick proclaimed, than the French turned their attention to securing, by garrisons, their claims to that vast territory which had been so hardily explored by La Salle and the adventurous missionaries; and in a short time a line of fortified posts was extended between the Gulf of St. Lawrence and the Gulf of Mexico. These territorial pretensions were not viewed, either in England or the colonies, without jealousy and alarm. The establishment of a fort by D'Ibberville, at the head of the Bay of Biloxi, in Louisiana, led to a memorial from Coxe, one of the proprietors of New Jersey, to the English king, praying that the settlement on the banks of the Mississippi might be encouraged.

So acceptable was the substance of this petition, that on its presentation William of Orange declared to his council, he "would leap over twenty stumbling-blocks rather than not effect it."

In 1701, war again broke out. It originated with the accession of a member of the Bourbon family to the throne of Spain. England had, therefore, on this occasion two nations opposed to her, and the southern provinces were now to be assailed by the Spaniards in Florida, while the French, of Canada and Acadie, continued their depredations on the eastern frontiers. An unsuccessful attempt made by Moore, the governor of South Carolina, against the Spanish town of St. Augustine, was the commencement of hostilities in that quarter. A new expedition took place in 1705, against the Spanish Indian settlements of the Apalachees. The villages were plundered, the churches robbed and burned, and the Indians, to the number of two thousand, removed to the banks of the Alatamaha.

In the meanwhile, the French were already desolating the frontiers of New England. On the 10th of August, 1703, detached parties of French and Indians assaulted, simultaneously, every settlement between Casco and Wells; sparing in their barbarous warfare, neither age nor infancy. In March, 1704, two hundred Canadians, and one hundred and fifty Indians, led by Hertelle de Rouville, marched over the snow from Canada, and fell suddenly upon the picketed village of Deersfield, then the northwestern frontier town of New England. In the early gray of morning, just as the sentinels had retired, they entered the palisades, rendered useless by the drifted snow, and raising the war-whoop, set the village in flames. But few of the inhabitants escaped, forty-seven were killed, and upwards of one hundred others, including the minister and his family, were taken captives. Then commenced, through that bitter wintry weather, the long, weary march to Canada. Two of the prisoners died of starvation by the way; while weak women and sorrowing children met their death by the tomahawk. A desultory warfare succeeded, and Massachusetts called upon the neighbouring colonies for assistance. A brief truce followed; but in 1707 the war was renewed. Another descent upon Acadie being determined on, a thousand men under Colonel March, sailed for Port Royal, and, supported by an English frigate, entered the river and landed before the town. This unfortunate settlement was again entirely destroyed; the houses were burned, the cattle killed, and the corn drowned by making openings in the embankments which protected the rich flats from the encroachments of the river. Being unprovided with heavy artillery, March retired to his vessels without attempting to assault the fort.

In retaliation for this foray, Hertelle de Rouville entered the valley of the Merrimac, and attacked Haverhill, the frontier settlement on that river. Assisted by his Indian allies, he plundered and burned the town, slew between forty and fifty of the inhabitants, led off as many more into captivity, and, though hotly pursued, succeeded in reaching Canada with the greater portion of his prisoners.

In 1710, Port Royal was again made the object of attack. Five hundred warriors and four regiments of militia from New England, under the command of Nicholson, the former governor of Virginia, sailed to attack the fort which March had not the means of assaulting with success. It was an easy conquest. The French garrison, feeble and mutinous, surrendered upon terms. Vetch, the second in command, was left with four hundred men to garrison the fort, which was soon after besieged by the Acadiens and Indians.

The following year, the English government fitted out a large fleet and army for the conquest of Canada. The command of this fleet, which consisted of fifteen ships of war, and forty transports, was given to Sir Hoveden Walker. Brigadier-general Masham was appointed to lead the troops, which comprised seven veteran regiments, and a battalion of marines. Through the incapacity of the admiral, this expedition—which was destined to attack Quebec, while a land force from Albany assaulted Montreal—ended in a most disastrous failure. On the 22d of August, eight of the vessels were wrecked in a fog among the Egg Islands of the St. Lawrence, and eight hundred and eighty-four men were drowned. Congratulating himself that, by this loss, he had been saved from venturing to Quebec, where the lives of many others might have been seriously jeopardized, Walker ordered the remaining vessels to put back; and in this shameful and inglorious manner ended an expedition, from which the most splendid results had been confidently anticipated.

CHAPTER XIX.

Treaty of Utrecht—Population of the Colonies—Absence of towns in Virginia—Crown Point taken possession of by the French—Communication between Canada and Louisiana—First newspaper in Virginia—War with Spain—Disastrous expedition to Carthagena—War with France—Capture of Louisburg—Treaty of Aix la Chapelle—Progress of Virginia—Religious intolerance—Capitol at Williamsburg burned—Close of Gooch's administration—Evidences of affectionate regard—Character of Gooch—Ohio Company—French claims—Opposite claims of the British—Brownsville founded—French posts established in the vicinity of the Ohio—Orders from England—Dinwiddie appointed Governor of Virginia—His purchase from the Indians—Back settlements of Virginia threatened by the French—A messenger despatched by Dinwiddie to ascertain their intentions—Virginia instructed to build two forts on the Ohio—George Washington—His early life and character.

The treaty of Utrecht in 1713, put an end to the second intercolonial war. On the battle fields of Europe, England had covered herself with glory, humbled the pride of the haughty Louis, and added fifty millions of pounds sterling to her national debt. Under the terms of the treaty, France ceded to England the territory of Hudson's Bay, the whole of New Foundland and Acadie, and the French part of the Island of St. Kitts, in the West Indies.

But, however distressing the second intercolonial war may have been to those families which settled the frontier towns, it had not checked in any considerable degree the increase of population. In 1715, the table compiled for the use of the Board of Trade, exhibited the whole population of the twelve colonies as four hundred and thirty-four thousand and six hundred. Virginia alone contained ninety-five thousand inhabitants, and yet there was not at this time, nor for many years after, any collection of houses in the whole province worthy to be dignified with the name of a town. In 1728, Norfolk was but a small commercial village, while Richmond was not founded until 1742, and at the commencement of the Revolution contained but a few straggling houses.

In 1729, two years after Gooch was appointed Governor of Virginia, a printing press was brought into the province, and in 1735, the first newspaper ever published in Virginia, was issued at Williamsburg.

No further interruption of consequence was experienced by the colonists until the year 1731, when the French sailed up Lake Champlain, and took possession of Crown Point, within one hundred miles of Albany. New York immediately sent a notice of this daring encroachment to the neighbouring states, and requested aid from England. But Walpole was resolutely bent on preserving peace, and the French were allowed to establish the new settlement without molestation.

The building of a fort at Niagara was regarded with an equal indifference.

As yet no French traders had approached the back settlements of Pennsylvania or Virginia. The easy communication existing between Lake Erie and the head waters of the Ohio appears at this time to have been unknown, the Wabash being regarded by the French as the main stream, to which the Ohio was but a tributary. Owing to an imperfect geographical knowledge of that region, the connection between Canada and Louisiana was kept up by the distant routes of Green Bay and Wisconsin, and subsequently, by way of the Maumee and the Wabash. When, however, the true character of the Ohio river became known, the facilities by which its waters could be reached from Lake Erie, tempted the French to fortify a post upon its banks, and by this means brought them into collision for the first time with the Virginians. This did not happen, however, until some years later. As yet, the vast region lying between the Ohio river and the great lakes remained a terra incognita to both nations.

In 1740, England having been forced into a war with Spain, all the North American colonies were called upon to aid in raising a regiment of thirty-five hundred men. The Assembly of Virginia responded to the call by increasing the duty on imported slaves to ten per cent., and by impressing the men of her quota from among the able-bodied idlers of the province.

The American levies were taken on board the fleet of Admiral Vernon, who sailed soon after from Jamaica to the assault of Carthagena, the strongest place in Spanish America. The result was melancholy in the extreme.

The attack, owing to differences between the military and naval commanders, was badly planned, and worse conducted. Some of the fortresses were taken, but that of San Lazaro, which commanded the town, was successfully defended by the Spaniards. The rainy season setting in soon after, the soldiers died by thousands, of the yellow fever. Vernon destroyed the fortifications, and retired to Jamaica. His entire losses were estimated at twenty thousand men. Of the troops furnished by the colonies, which, including five hundred additional men subsequently furnished by Massachusetts, amounted to four thousand, only four hundred returned to their homes.

The Spaniards thus triumphantly freed from an expedition, the magnitude of which had been a well grounded source of alarm, now retaliated by precipitating a large force upon the infant province of Georgia. By the signal ability of General Oglethorpe the invaders were repulsed, and after failing in their attack on Frederica, they hurriedly re-embarked on board their vessels, and returned to Cuba.

The war with France against Austria, speedily involved England, as the ally of the latter. In 1744, France again declared war with England. The first intimation received by the colonies of the recommencement of hostilities in North America, was the capture of Fort Canso, in Nova Scotia, by a party of Canadians. At the same time the Indians began to lay desolate the frontiers of Maine.

Shirley, the Governor of Massachusetts, immediately bestirred himself. The legislature of the province determined by a majority of one vote to attempt the capture of Louisburg, the strongest fortress north of the Gulf of Mexico. New York and Pennsylvania sent supplies of artillery and provisions. The New England provinces furnished the necessary troops. Assisted by the British squadron, under Commodore Warren, the forces from New England, after a siege of six weeks, compelled the garrison to capitulate, and the inhabitants of Cape Breton immediately acknowledged allegiance to England.

The news of this important success was rapidly conveyed by expresses to the governors of the various English colonies. Virginia at once generously threw open her ports for the purposes of trade, free of all duty, to vessels sailing from the newly acquired island of Cape Breton, and the governor despatched to Louisburg, for the use of the garrison, provisions to the value of two thousand pounds.

But the war which had been thus recommenced, was carried on languidly by both nations, and in America had only affected the extreme frontiers, when it was brought to a close in 1748, by the treaty of Aix la Chapelle.

Four years previous to this, while the New England provinces were preparing for the expedition to Louisburg, Virginia was extending her borders by a treaty with deputies from the Six Nations. For about four hundred pounds, a deed was obtained from the chiefs of the Iroquois, to all the territory beyond the mountains, that was then, or should be hereafter considered by the King of England as belonging to the colony of Virginia.

Subject to none of those hostile invasions by which the peace of the extreme north and south had been so often disturbed, the population of Virginia continued steadily to increase, until at length her settlements extended beyond the mountains west of the blue ridge.

The attachment of the Virginians to the doctrines of the Church of England had frequently rendered them intolerant of the religious tenets of others. Even the mild, gentlemanly, and exemplary Gooch, was not free from this narrow spirit. In his address to the grand jury in April,

1745, he recommended to their attention certain false teachers lately crept into the province, who, without order or license, or producing any testimonial of their education, or sect, had "led the innocent and ignorant people into all kinds of delusion." How far the presentments of the grand jury conformed to the spirit of this address has not been ascertained; but that the worthy, though prejudiced governor, expressed the sentiments of a great majority of the Virginians of that day, there does not exist the shadow of a doubt.

During the year following, the public buildings at Williamsburg being reduced to ashes, the subject began to be agitated of removing the seat of government to some point more advantageously situated in the heart, rather than near the extremity of the province.

The members of the Assembly entered warmly upon the subject of removal, and in a speech to the governor eulogized the foundation of a new central city in the most glowing terms. "To lay the foundation of a new city," said they, "to raise a capitol in a place commodiously situated for navigation, will complete the glory of your administration, and transmit your name with the highest lustre to future ages. With what pleasure may we then extend our view through future centuries, and anticipate the happiness provided for posterity."

This very respectful, but somewhat inflated language, had no effect on the old governor. The best houses in Williamsburg were owned by himself, by the members of his council, and by gentlemen of importance in the colony. This property would necessarily diminish in value by the proposed change. The influence of the college, and that of other officers of government, was also thrown into the scale of opposition, so that Williamsburg, notwithstanding many wordy altercations, remained the capital of the province up to the period of the Revolutionary war.

In 1749, the administration of Gooch, which for upwards of twenty-two years had been of the most courteous character, was terminated by his departure for England. The sixth and last colonial revisal of the Virginia code took place only a short time previous to his leaving the province.

When Governor Gooch was about to set sail, he was honoured by the president and council with an address significant of their profound appreciation of the many blessings they had enjoyed under his wise and benificent government, and their sincere respect for his public and private virtues. The collegiate authorities of William and Mary, and the municipality of Williamsburg expressed a similar sense of his merits, and the good old governor finally embarked amidst the tears and benedictions of the people, among whom he had lived so long, and over whom he had exercised a sway that might justly be regarded as paternal.

The courtesy of Governor Gooch has been handed down to the present time in the shape of an anecdote, which well illustrates the character of a true gentleman. Having been reproached one day for returning the salutation of a negro, Gooch replied mildly, "I should be much ashamed that a negro should have better manners than I." A baronetcy was the reward of his long and faithful services to a province whose people always spoke of him with affection, and justly regarded him as one of their warmest and most steadfast friends.

The government now devolved on Robinson, the president of the council; but on his death a few days afterward, Thomas Lee, as president, succeeded to the administration.

During the brief deputy-governorship of Lee, surveyors were permitted to measure and locate lands on the other side of the mountains, provided they did not interfere with grants made to the Ohio Company. Before November, 1750, the period to which the Assembly stood prorogued, Lee died, and was succeeded by Lewis Burwell.

The Ohio Company, of which mention has already been made, consisted of an association of London merchants and Virginia land speculators. This company had obtained in England, shortly after the treaty of Aix la Chapelle, a grant of six hundred thousand acres of land, on the east branch of the Ohio river, greatly to the indignation of the French, who claimed by right of discovery the entire region watered by the Mississippi and its tributaries. The British opposed to the claims of the French those of the Six Nations, who asserted the territory to have become theirs by right of conquest, and had already sold a portion of it to Virginia under that title. The French pointed to the numerous posts and garrisons, more than sixty in number, which they had maintained on the lakes, the Mississippi, and the Wabash, for a number of years. Their title was complete enough to the country on the upper lakes, the Mississippi, the Illinois, and the Wabash, while to render it valid to the territory immediately south of Lake Erie, the Count de la Galisonniére, Governor-general of Canada, despatched an officer with three hundred men, to spread themselves over the country lying between Detroit and the Cumberland Mountains, to bury at the most important points leaden plates, engraved with the arms of France, to take possession of the territory with a formal process verbal, and to warn English traders out of the country.

In 1752, the Ohio Company built a trading house and fort at Brownsville, on the Monongahela. This act gave great offence to the French, who made a descent upon the Miami Indians, settled at Sandusky, and burned their village because they persisted in trading with the English.

Early in 1753, twelve hundred men from Montreal built a fort at Presque Isle, on the southern shore of Lake Erie, and then, moving southward, established posts on French Creek, and the main stream of the Alleghany.

The Board of Trade reported these encroachments upon Pennsylvania and Virginia to the king, and orders were immediately sent to the colonial governors to repel force by force, whenever the French were found within the undoubted limits of their provinces.

During the year 1752, Robert Dinwiddie, previously a member of the council, and surveyor-general of the colonial customs, succeeded Burwell as deputy-governor of Virginia. Conscious that the movements of the French toward the upper waters of the Ohio, seriously threatened the back settlements of Virginia, Dinwiddie purchased from the Indians on the Monongahela permission to build a fort at the junction of that river with the Alleghany. Tidings reaching the capital of Virginia soon after, that the French were about to establish fortifications on the Ohio, and that the Indian tribes in the surrounding region exhibited symptoms of hostility, it was thought necessary to send a messenger over the mountains, with instructions to ascertain the temper and designs of the Indians, and to make himself acquainted with the movements and intentions of the French. The first messenger sent out, failing to execute his mission perfectly, and orders having, in the mean time, reached Governor Dinwiddie from England to build two forts on the Ohio, for which artillery and ammunition had been sent out, it was thought advisable to send a commissioner in due form, and invested with proper credentials, to confer with the officer in command of the French forces; to ascertain under what authority he was acting, and what were his ulterior designs. This delicate and dangerous mission was entrusted to George Washington, the eldest son of a widowed mother, a surveyor by profession; and although at this time but twenty-one years of age, already distinguished for his judgment and capacity, and the purity of his moral character. Born on the old ancestral domain in Westmoreland county, he was removed in infancy to the banks of the Rappahannock, where he became an orphan in his eleventh year.

In 1743, his father, Augustine Washington, a farmer in affluent circumstances, died, leaving a competent provision for his widow and children. Growing up thus under the care of his mother, the youthful Washington, whose name was soon to become a household word in the history of a great nation, received only such common education as the indifferent schools of the neighbourhood at that time afforded. To read, to write, and to cipher, composed the whole of his knowledge. To add to the means derived from his paternal estate, he studied the lucrative profession of a surveyor, and at the age of sixteen entered upon its arduous and toilsome duties in the rich valleys of the Alleghany mountains.

The careful accuracy with which these his earliest surveys were made soon brought him into notice, and established his reputation. The following year he received a commission as a public surveyor, and passed the three subsequent years among the southern branches of the Potomac river, and the spurs and ridges of the Alleghanies. In addition to this employment, he had been appointed, at the age of nineteen, military inspector of one of the districts into which the province was divided, with the rank of major; a commission which must have been peculiarly gratifying to one whose military predilections had always been of the strongest character, and had hitherto only been subdued by the force of prudential considerations.

It was while engaged in the performance of the duties belonging to this office, that Major Washington was selected by Dinwiddie to proceed to the French posts in the vicinity of the Ohio.

His instructions were to travel without delay to the Ohio river. To halt at a place called Logstown, and after convening some of the principal Indian chiefs of the vicinity, to learn where the French were stationed, and obtain an escort of warriors to that point. On his arrival at the principal French post, he was to present his credentials, and demand an answer. He was also to make secret inquiry into the number of French troops, and the prospect of reinforcements from Canada; what forts they had erected, how they were garrisoned, and their distances from each other.

Furnished with a passport, and these instructions, Washington left Williamsburg on the thirty-first of October, 1753. The distance he had to traverse was nearly six hundred miles, a great part over lofty and rugged mountains, and more than half of the way through wild forests, never trodden before by any human feet but those of the white hunter and the wandering savage.

CHAPTER XX.

Mission of Washington to the Ohio—Reaches Will's Creek—Halts at the Forks of the Ohio—Holds a conference with Indians at Logstown—Delivers his letter and credentials to the French commandant—His return—Is shot at by an Indian—His peril in crossing the Alleghany river—Arrives at Williamsburg—Increase of the provincial army—Washington appointed lieutenant-colonel—Marches to Will's Creek—The French drive off the troops at the Forks of the Ohio, and build Fort Duquesne—Skirmish at Great Meadows—Death of Jumonville, and capture of his party—Fort Necessity erected—Invested by the French—The Virginians capitulate on terms—Washington resigns his commission and retires to private life—Arrival of General Braddock with troops from England—Is joined by Washington as a volunteer—March of the army—Crossing of the Alleghanies—Defeat of Braddock on the banks of the Monongahela—Death of Braddock—Heroism of the Virginia troops—Retreat of the army to Cumberland.

ACCOMPANIED by John Davidson, an Indian interpreter, and Jacob Vanbraam, engaged in consequence of his knowledge of the French language, Major Washington, travelling by way of Fredericksburg, Alexandria, and Winchester, reached Will's Creek in fourteen days. At this point Fort Cumberland was subsequently erected. Here he was joined by Mr. Gist, a person well acquainted with the route to the Ohio river, who consented to act as guide. Four attendants, two of whom were Indian traders, were also added to the party.

From the frontier station of Will's Creek, Washington and his party passed over the Alleghanies, already covered with snow. The swollen and turbulent streams that intercepted their way, were crossed by means of rafts, or by swimming their horses. When they reached the junction of the Monongahela with the Alleghany, the point at which Dinwiddie had, by purchase of the Indians, obtained the right to build a fort, Washington narrowly examined the ground, and on his return home reported to the governor his opinion of its advantages as a military post. Upon his recommendation a fort was subsequently commenced on the site then chosen, the walls of which were in the slow process of erection, when the workmen were driven off by the advance of the French.

Proceeding thence, on the main purpose of his mission, to Logstown, twenty miles below the forks of the Ohio, as the point of junction between the Monongahela and the Alleghany was at that time called, Washington held a conference with some of the neighbouring Indian chiefs, and requested a guard of friendly warriors to the nearest French post. The principal sachem, Tanacharison, and four other Indians, finally agreed to accompany him.

The head-quarters of the French commandant were one hundred and twenty miles distant, but at the nearer outpost of Venango, Washington was treated with civility by Captain Joncaire, and directed on his way, although many subtle efforts were made to detach the Indians from his service.

At the end of forty-one days from the time of his leaving Williamsburg, Washington found himself in the presence of M. de St. Pierre, the French commandant, to whom he presented his commission, and the letter of Governor Dinwiddie. The reply of the commandant was courteous but decided. In all that he had done, he said, having acted under the instructions of the Marquis Du Quesne, Governor of Canada, the summons to retire could not be complied with.

His mission being thus fulfilled, Washington, sending his horses overland, embarked with the rest of his companions, in a canoe, and floated down French Creek, through drifting ice, to the outpost of Venango, a distance of one hundred and thirty miles, which was accomplished with difficulty in six days, they being at one time obliged to avoid the packed ice, by carrying the heavy canoe across a neck of land a quarter of a mile over.

The embarrassment of the journey, owing to the ruggedness of the way, and the inclemency of the wintry weather, at length determined Washington to proceed on foot, clad in an Indian walking dress, and bearing on his back a knapsack containing his papers and food. Mr. Gist accompanied him, equipped in a similar manner. On the south-east fork of Beaver Creek, the travellers met with an Indian, who called Gist by his name, and who on being asked the nearest route to the forks of the Alleghany, consented to act as a guide. He relieved Major Washington of his knapsack, and for eight or ten miles travelled with them, when Washington, growing weary and foot-sore, desired to encamp. The Indian then offered to carry his gun, but this being prudently declined, he grew churlish, and advised them to keep on until they reached his cabin, as there were Ottowa Indians in the wood who would scalp them if they lay out.

With increasing distrust of their savage guide, the travellers proceeded two miles further, when Washington declared his determination to halt at the next water. As soon as they reached an open clearing, the Indian paused suddenly, turned about at a distance of fifteen paces, and fired. Fortunately, both Washington and his companion remained unharmed. Gist immediately took the treacherous savage prisoner, and would have killed him, but for the humane interposition of Washington, who kept him a close prisoner until nine o'clock that evening, and then set him free. He had no sooner bounded fairly out of sight than the travellers set a compass, and having fixed their course, walked briskly all night to put themselves beyond reach of pursuit.

The next afternoon, at dusk, they reached the Alleghany, a little above Shannopins. From want of means to cross the river they were compelled to encamp on its banks, with no other covering but their blankets to protect them from the snow.

When the morning came, there was no way of getting over but on a raft; which they set about constructing, with but one poor hatchet, and finished just after sunsetting. This was a whole day's work. Launching the raft at once, they stepped on board, and immediately pushed from the shore. They had scarcely reached the middle of the river before they were jammed in the ice, in such a manner that they expected every moment the raft would sink. To save themselves from this danger, Washington put out his setting pole, and attempted to stop the raft until the ice should pass by; but the rapidity of the stream threw the raft with so much violence against the pole, that he was jerked off into ten feet water. Fortunately, he saved himself by catching hold of one of the raft logs. Notwithstanding all their efforts, they could not reach either shore, but were compelled to desert their raft, and take refuge on an island in the river. On this desolate spot, chilled, helpless, and suffering dreadfully from frozen feet and hands, they passed the night. With the dawn of morning the prospect of escape opened. The ice in the river had congealed sufficiently strong to bear their weight, and passing over without accident, they finally reached the trading post of a Mr. Frazier, on the Monongahela. After remaining there three days to recruit their strength, and procure horses, they recrossed the Alleghanies to Will's Creek. At this point Washington parted with Mr. Gist, and continued his journey alone to Williamsburg, where he arrived on the 16th of January, 1754, after an absence of eleven weeks.

Dinwiddie immediately convened the assembly. The report of Washington placing the intentions of the French beyond doubt, the burgesses granted ten thousand pounds towards the defence of the frontiers, but encroached upon the prerogative of the governor by appointing a committee to supervise the expenditure of the money. Dinwiddie was excessively annoyed at the independent spirit displayed by the assembly on this occasion. Writing subsequently to the Earl of Holdernesse, he says, "I am sorry to find them very much in a republican way of thinking; and indeed they do not act in a proper constitutional way, but make encroachments on the prerogative of the crown, to which some former governors have submitted too much to them; and I fear, without a very particular instruction, it will be difficult to bring them to order."

The military force of Virginia was speedily increased to six hundred men. Of this regiment, Joshua Fry was appointed colonel, and Washington lieutenant-colonel. Three independent companies of colonial troops, in the pay of Great Britain, and commanded by officers holding commissions from the crown, were ordered from New York and South Carolina, to assist in the operations against the enemy; while North Carolina voted twelve thousand pounds, and promised to send a body of troops as early as they could be enlisted.

During the early part of April, 1754, Washington, whose head-quarters had been at Alexandria, marched from that place with two companies—subsequently reinforced on his route by a third—to Will's Creek, where he arrived on the 20th of the same month.

A party of forty-one men under Captain Trent, had already been thrown forward to the forks of the Ohio, where they commenced building the fort which Washington had previously recommended should be constructed at that place. The latter had scarcely reached Will's Creek, before he received intelligence that a body of French troops, to the number of one thousand men, had descended the river from Venango, with eighteen pieces of cannon, sixty batteaux, and three hundred canoes, under the command of Captain Contrecœur; had taken forcible possession of the unfinished fort, dismissed the Virginia troops at work upon it, and completing the works themselves, had called them Fort Duquesne, in honour of the governor-general of Canada.

This was the first open act of hostility. After holding a council of war, Washington hastily pressed forward with his detachment, in the hope of being able to penetrate to the mouth of Red Stone Creek, on the Monongahela, where he designed erecting a fortification for the protection of his troops, until the reinforcements he had sent for should arrive.

At the passage of the Youghiogany, he was warned by his old friend Tanacharison of the approach of a French detachment, the commander of which had expressed a determination to attack the first English they should meet. After throwing up an entrenchment at a place called the Great Meadows, Washington sent forward a party of soldiers, mounted on wagon horses, to reconnoitre; but they returned without having discovered traces of the enemy. Mr. Gist came in soon after, and reported the presence of fifty French soldiers at his settlement the day previous. At nine o'clock the same night another express arrived from Tanacharison, stating that the French detachment was near his camp, a distance of six miles from Great Meadows.

Taking with him forty men, Washington immediately marched to form a junction with his

Indian allies. After having been baffled for six hours by the narrowness of the trails, which were continually being lost amidst the heavy blinding rains and the darkness of the night, he reached the Indian encampment on the 28th of May, a little before sunrise. Upon consultation with Tanacharison and other chiefs, it was resolved to march against the French at once. Two Indians were accordingly sent forward to reconnoitre the position of the enemy, who reported them as engaged in pitching their tents, about half a mile from the road, in a valley surrounded by rocks. Arrangements were immediately made to attack them on all sides. It was accomplished most effectually. As soon as the Virginians were dis covered, the French seized their pieces and formed; but when they found themselves exposed to a fire in front and rear, they threw down their arms. In this brief skirmish the French sustained a los of ten killed, one wounded, and twenty-one taken prisoners. Only a single man escaped. Among the killed was Jumonville, the commander of the detachment. The principal officers taken, were M. Drouillon and M. La Force, the latter of whom Washington speaks of in his despatch as "a bold, enterprising man, and a person of great subtlety and cunning."

The skirmish at Great Meadows, on account of its occurring before war was formally declared between England and France, created a great sensation, especially in the latter country. The conduct of Washington was strongly censured. The death of Jumonville was regarded at Paris in the light of a ferocious murder. He was there represented as a peaceful messenger, who had been suddenly waylaid and assassinated, in a manner contrary to all the rules of war established among civilized nations.

The reply of Washington to these denunciations was brief, but pertinent. "Instead of coming in the public and open manner of ambassadors, the party of Jumonville came secretly; they sought out the most hidden retreats, and remained concealed whole days within five miles of us. After sending out spies to reconnoitre our position, they retreated two miles, from whence they sent messengers to M. Contrecœur, with the results of their reconnoisance." The deserters who subsequently joined the force under Washington, corroborated these statements. They asserted that Jumonville, though sent out ostensibly as the bearer of a summons warning the English to retire beyond the Alleghanies, was in reality engaged in the duties of a spy, having orders to present his summons only in the event of falling in with a superior party.

Having forwarded his prisoners, and being strengthened by a reinforcement of troops, Washington, now elevated to the chief command by the death of Colonel Fry, erected a stockade fort at Great Meadows, to which he gave the name of Fort Necessity. Leaving a garrison at this point under charge of Captain Mackay, he pushed on towards Fort Duquesne, but was soon obliged to fall back before a superior force of the enemy. He had scarcely returned to Fort Necessity before the imperfect works were invested by fifteen hundred French and Indians, commanded by M. de Villier. After a brief but spirited defence, the fort was surrendered, on condition that the garrison should be permitted to retire with their arms and baggage. The following morning the Virginians marched out of the fort, and bearing the wounded on their backs, proceeded to Will's Creek, where they assisted in building Fort Cumberland.

Changes in the organization of the army having been subsequently introduced by Governor Dinwiddie, Washington resigned his commission, and retired to private life.

Early in the spring of 1755, General Braddock arrived in Virginia with two regiments of regulars, and encamped at Alexandria. This strong force, aided by the colonial militia, was supposed to be amply sufficient to drive the French across the Canadian frontiers. At the urgent request of Braddock, Colonel Washington consented to take part in the campaign as a member of his military family.

The army commenced its march soon after,

reaching Winchester about the twentieth of April. From thence the troops marched by different routes to Fort Cumberland, the extreme frontier settlement. At this point they were reinforced by one thousand Virginians. The inability of the contractors to supply the necessary means of transporting the provisions and artillery across the mountains, occasioned great vexation to the commanding general, and delayed for some time the progress of the troops. These embarrassments were at length overcome by the energy and activity of Franklin, then postmaster-general for the colonies.

On the 10th of June, the vanguard of the army was once more in motion. Having now to encounter the steep rough ridges of the Alleghanies, over which a road had to be cut with great labour for the wagons and artillery, the march was slow and difficult in the extreme. Three days were occupied in accomplishing but six of the fifty miles which lay between Fort Cumberland and Redstone, on the Monongahela. Conscious that if these delays continued, the season would be consumed in crossing the mountains, Braddock, acting upon the advice of Washington, separated the army into two divisions, and leaving Colonel Dunbar to bring up the heavy baggage, pushed forward, in advance, at the head of twelve hundred men lightly equipped.

A sickness, brought on by fatigue of body and

mind, confined Washington to the rear division for nearly two weeks. Anxious, however, to be at his post before the army reached Fort Duquesne, he parted from the troops under Dunbar, and, borne by short stages across the mountains, overtook Braddock fifteen miles from Fort Duquesne, the evening before the battle of Monongahela.

The British general had been repeatedly warned of the danger to which he was exposed from the wild and rugged character of the country, and the peculiar method of savage warfare. It was suggested to him to employ the three companies of provincials, forming part of the first division, as rangers, to scour the country in advance of the army; but Braddock, wedded to a system of European tactics, and despising alike Frenchmen, provincials, and Indians, adhered to arrangements which, however suitable they might have been on the broad plains of Europe, were in the last degree pedantic and mischievous among the intricate forests of America. Early on the morning of the ninth of July, 1755, the army crossed the Monongahela, a little below the mouth of the Youghiogany, and after marching till about noon, forded the river a second time at a distance of about ten miles from Fort Duquesne. When they reached the northern bank of the Monongahela, three hundred men, commanded by Colonel Gage, were thrown forward, supported at a little distance, by a party of two hundred, ordered to act as a reserve. These latter were followed by the main body, commanded by Braddock in person, which being encumbered with baggage and artillery, moved but slowly. The whole army had scarcely left the bank of the river, before a sharp firing was heard in front and on the left flank, and the main body hastened up to the support of their companions. But before they could succeed in doing this, the advanced parties fell back successively in great confusion, and breaking through the main body, so thoroughly disorganized it, that no after efforts on the part of the general and his officers could restore them to order. In this state, huddled together in dense masses, firing panic stricken at the concealed enemy, and often shooting down their own officers and men, the regulars remained for three hours. It was in vain that Braddock exerted himself to form his men into platoons and columns. The French and Indians, protected by ravines and high bushes on each side of the road, poured from their places of concealment a continuous fire, by which sixty officers and nearly seven hundred men, or one-half of the whole force engaged, were either killed or wounded. Braddock himself had five horses shot under him, and fell soon after wounded mortally. His two aids had already been borne disabled from the field. The regulars now gave way on all sides, and the flight soon became a perfect rout. The Virginia troops alone, by taking to the trees and fighting after the Indian manner, behaved with a courage and coolness worthy of their old reputation. Washington, still feeble from his recent illness, placed himself at their head, and covered for a time the disorderly retreat of the regulars. At length the brave provincials were cut to pieces. Of three companies which were in the action, only thirty men escaped. Washington, though always in the thickest of the fight, miraculously escaped unharmed, though he had two horses shot under him, and four bullets had pierced his clothes.

So thoroughly disorganized were the fugitive regulars, that it was found impossible to rally them until they reached the rear division under Dunbar. On the 13th of June, the brave, but arrogant, Braddock, expired of his wounds, and was buried on the road near Fort Necessity. The panic among the soldiers still continuing, Dunbar abandoned the expedition, and after destroying his artillery and stores, retreated across the mountains to Fort Cumberland, and from thence to Philadelphia.

The campaign being thus brought to a disastrous close, Colonel Washington, after resting a few days at the fort to recruit his strength, returned to Mount Vernon, an estate belonging to the orphan daughter of his deceased brother

Lawrence, but which subsequently descended to himself, as heir at law.

CHAPTER XXI.

Indian incursions—Activity of Washington—Dinwiddie convenes the assembly—Increase of troops—Washington appointed commander-in-chief—Hastens to Winchester—Distressed condition of the settlers—His letter to the governor—His painful situation—Fort Loudoun commenced—England declares war against France—Arrival of the Earl of Loudoun—Success of the French under Montcalm—Conference at Philadelphia—Plan of the campaign—Failure of the expedition against Louisburg—Campaign of 1758—Energetic measures of Pitt—Expedition ordered against Fort Duquesne—Advance of Colonel Bouquet—The Virginia troops concentrated at Fort Cumberland—A new road opened to Loyal Hanna—A detachment under Major Grant ordered to reconnoitre Fort Duquesne—Defeat of Grant—Arrival of General Forbes at Loyal Hanna—Council of war—Advance of the troops—The fort burned and deserted by the French—Fort Pitt erected on its site—Campaign of 1759—Treaty of Fontainbleau.

EMBOLDENED by their success in defeating the army under Braddock, the French Indians no longer confined their hostile incursions to the settlements on the frontiers. They crossed the mountains, and after spreading themselves over the country in the vicinity of Fort Cumberland, penetrated to within twenty miles of Winchester. Wherever they moved they committed the most horrible atrocities. Whole families of settlers were massacred, scouting parties were cut off, and even the fortified stations attacked, with a boldness that was increased by the feebleness with which they were opposed.

Although he had resigned his commission of colonel in the service of Virginia, Washington still retained the office of adjutant-general of militia. Fully conscious that nothing but the most energetic measures could save the inhabitants of the frontiers from being utterly extirpated by their savage and barbarous enemies, he called out the militia for exercise and review, and encouraged the formation of volunteer companies.

Equally impressed with the necessity of immediate action in a crisis already so imminent, Governor Dinwiddie convened the assembly on the 4th of August. The session, which was brief, resulted in a vote of forty thousand pounds for the public service, and authority to increase the Virginia regiment to sixteen companies.

The organization of this body was entrusted to Washington, with the commission of commander-in-chief of all the forces raised, and to be raised, in Virginia, and the unusual privilege of naming his own field officers. He had scarcely set out on his journey to Williamsburg, for the purpose of conferring with the governor upon a plan of operations, when he was overtaken by an express announcing a new and more destructive irruption of the French and Indians, and was compelled to hasten to Winchester.

His personal presence abated in some degree the terrors which the sanguinary excesses of the enemy had inspired. He collected and armed the men who had fled with their families from scenes of desolation and carnage, and directed the county lieutenants, and the officers engaged in enlisting volunteers, to concentrate their recruits and militia, as speedily as possible, at Winchester. Before these orders could be executed, the enemy had recrossed the Alleghanies with their prisoners and plunder. No pursuit was made. The number of regular troops employed in the service of Virginia was totally insufficient for the protection of so extensive a frontier, and effective service was found impracticable from the militia.

Deeply affected by the distresses of the inhabitants, and the constant recurrence of barbarities on the part of the savages, for which he could afford no relief beyond uncertain promises, Washington wrote a most pathetic letter to the governor, urging the assembly to more vigorous measures. In this letter he says, "The supplicating tears of the women, and moving petitions of the men, melt me with such deadly sorrow, that I solemnly declare, if I know my own mind, I could offer myself a willing sacrifice to the butchering enemy, provided that would contribute to the people's ease."

As the only remedy for disasters which threatened, otherwise, the inevitable destruction of all the forts, stations, and settlements, between the Ohio River and the Blue Ridge, Washington proposed a new organization of the militia, and an increase of the regular troops. His suggestions being only partially adopted by the assembly, he was reduced, to his great chagrin, to a system of defensive operations; the duties of which were both harassing and inglorious, and the summer of 1756 was wasted in a series of petty skirmishes, entailing great loss of life upon the troops engaged in them, without being effectual in repressing the incursions of the enemy.

This unhappy state of things excited feelings of the most painful emotion in the breast of Washington, who was compelled, on the one hand, to listen to murmurs of discontent from his own soldiers, and on the other, to heart-rending appeals for protection from the distressed inhabitants. His situation was rendered still more unenviable by the conduct of the governor, who, without possessing any military knowledge, undertook to regulate the principal operations. Whilst yielding obedience to orders that were found practicable, Washington protested warmly against being made responsible for military movements over which he had no control. His fine sense of honour was subject to a yet keener annoyance in the rumours which were circulated at this period, by certain friends of the governor, to the disparagement of the army, charging the officers with gross irregularities and neglect of duty, and indirectly throwing the blame upon the commander. Justly indignant at being made the object of accusations as false as they were slanderous, his first impulse was to resign his commission and retire from the service; but his half-formed purpose was speedily overruled by the remonstrances of his friends, the general voice of the people, and by his own high sense of the duty which he owed to his native province.

The expected arrival of the Earl of Loudoun to take command of the royal forces in America—a station temporarily occupied, since the fall of Braddock, by Governor Shirley of Massachusetts—may also have had its effect in reconciling Washington to bear, with such patience as he might, the annoyances to which he was subjected.

Hoping soon to be called upon to take part in a campaign of a more decided character, he busied himself, in the mean while, in strengthening the old forts and constructing new ones. A fort was also commenced at Winchester, as a depository for military stores, and a rallying point for such settlers as might be driven in from the frontiers. It was called Loudoun, in honour of the new commander-in-chief.

On the 18th of May, 1756, England formally declared war against France, and, late in July, the Earl of Loudoun arrived in America. He had scarcely assumed the duties of his command, before intelligence was brought him that the Marquis Montcalm had captured, after a short bombardment, the strong fort of Oswego, and taken its garrison, consisting of more than a thousand men, prisoners of war.

The expedition previously planned against Ticonderoga and Crown Point was immediately abandoned; the troops which were on the march to reinforce the garrison at Oswego, fell back in dismay to Albany; the militia were suffered to return to their homes; and, as the season was by this time well advanced, the regulars were ordered into winter quarters at New York and Albany.

In March, 1757, Washington attended a meeting of governors and officers at Philadelphia, which had been convened by Loudoun for the purpose of arranging with them the plan of the ensuing campaign. Washington urged his favourite project of an expedition against Duquesne; but it was finally decided to continue the system of defensive operations in the middle and southern states, while the main army directed its efforts against the garrisons of the enemy at Louisburg and upon the lakes.

Through the tardiness and indecision of the commander-in-chief, the expedition organized against Louisburg resulted in a complete failure. In the mean time, the energetic Montcalm placed himself at the head of eight thousand men, and invested Fort William Henry at the southern extremity of Lake George. After a siege of six days the garrison, consisting of two thousand men, having exhausted their ammunition, capitulated on condition of being suffered to march out with the honours of war.

On the frontiers of Virginia the Indians still continued their predatory inroads, almost with impunity.

Washington had returned to his old quarters at Winchester; but little could be done beyond maintaining the garrisons already established, and alleviating the sufferings of those who had fled from the fury of the savages. It was well understood by this time that no scheme of effectual relief could be planned, which had not for its basis the capture of Fort Duquesne.

The close of the year 1757 saw the French in possession of all their fortresses, from Cape Breton to Louisiana; while they had expelled the English from Oswego and Lake George, and had reduced the Six Nations to a position of neutrality.

The campaign of 1758, was to open under happier auspices. The elder Pitt had taken his seat in the British cabinet, as secretary of state, and understanding, far better than his predecessors, the importance and condition of the American provinces, he resolved on a vigorous prosecution of the war, the plan of which embraced a series of offensive operations throughout the frontiers.

To the great joy of Virginia, General Forbes was ordered to undertake the conquest of Fort Duquesne. Thoroughly appreciating the inability of the provinces to carry on the war to a successful conclusion at their own expense, Pitt addressed a circular to the respective governors, requesting them to raise an aggregate force of not less than twenty thousand men, and offering to reimburse the expense of the levies by a subsequent parliamentary grant. The troops thus raised were to be armed and provisioned at the charge of the crown. The effect of this liberality was at once apparent. Massachusetts, Connecticut, Rhode Island, New Hampshire, New York, New Jersey, and Pennsylvania, promptly responded to the call of the energetic minister.

The forces in Virginia were immediately increased to two regiments of a thousand men each. Colonel Washington, still retaining his commission as commander-in-chief of the Virginia troops, was placed at the head of the first regiment. The command of the second was given to Colonel Byrd.

In the mean while, the affairs of the province had been materially benefited by a change of governors. Dinwiddie had sailed for England in

January, 1758, leaving behind him a character for arrogance and avarice, which made his departure a source of congratulation rather than of regret. Lord Loudoun had been appointed to succeed him; but the pressure of his military duties detaining him at the north, John Blair, president of the council, acted as chief magistrate until the 7th of June, when he surrendered his authority into the hands of the newly commissioned governor, Francis Fauquier.

The period at length approached when the long wished for movement against Fort Duquesne was to take place. The army appointed to effect the conquest of this important fortress amounted to seven thousand men. General Forbes being taken ill on his way from Philadelphia, the regulars and Pennsylvania troops, commanded by Colonel Bouquet, were ordered in advance to Raystown, on the south branch of the Juniata; and early in July, the Virginia regiments under Washington, were concentrated at Fort Cumberland. During the absence of General Forbes, scouting parties, clothed in the light Indian dress, were employed in opening a road to Raystown, thirty miles distant, and in repairing the one leading to Great Meadows. Differences of opinion arising in relation to the line of route, Washington strenuously urged that the troops should march from Cumberland, over the road previously constructed by the army under Braddock. His advice was disregarded. A new road was ordered to be commenced from Raystown, as the nearest and most direct route to the Ohio. For six weeks Bouquet's advance division of twenty-five hundred men were kept incessantly employed on this arduous service, and on the 10th of September had penetrated no further than Loyal Hanna, a distance of forty-five miles from Raystown. While two-thirds of the troops were employed in constructing a fort at this point, Colonel Bouquet sent forward Major Grant, with a detachment of eight hundred men, to reconnoitre the country in the vicinity of Fort Duquesne.

On the fourteenth of September, after a march of nearly fifty miles, Grant reached a hill overlooking the fort. Under cover of the night, he drew up his men in the order of battle, and advanced a small party of observation. Early the following morning, he ordered Major Lewis to take command of the baggage guard, and fall back some two miles in the rear. At the same time he sent an engineer, with a covering party, to take a plan of the works. To crown his rashness, he ordered the reveille to be beaten by all the drums in the detachment.

The fort remained sternly silent. Not a single gun was fired, not a single sound of preparation was heard within its walls. This ominous stillness Grant attributed to fear. He was soon to be terribly undeceived. All at once, the gates were flung open, and multitudes of Indians came streaming out, brandishing their weapons, and startling the air with the shrillness of the war-whoop. Spreading themselves on the flanks of the covering party, they sent from the shelter of trees and high grass, and from behind boulders of rock, and the undulations of the ground, a perfect storm of bullets; while a chosen body of French regulars advanced in close order, and commenced an attack in front. Grant descended the hill to the support of his detachment, but they were killed almost to a man before he reached them. The main body, fighting in masses, soon began to suffer terribly under the spirited attacks of the French and the more deadly fire of the concealed savages. They were speedily thrown into disorder, but still fought with a blind fury, which injured the enemy but little, while it brought destruction upon themselves. Early in the action, Major Lewis hastened to the assistance of Grant, with the greater portion of his rear guard, leaving Captain Bullet with fifty men for the defence of the baggage. This reinforcement proved utterly ineffectual in checking the success of the enemy. The Indians, now confident of victory, sprang from their coverts, and assaulted the wavering troops with the tomahawk and the scalping knife. They gave no quarter; but inhumanly butchered the regulars and provincials in the very act of surrender. Grant barely succeeded in saving his life by capitulating to a French officer. Lewis, after defending himself with great gallantry from the attacks of several savages, one of whom he killed, was forced to retreat upon a French detachment and yield himself a prisoner of war. On the capture of their principal officers, the troops fled from the field in complete rout. Following close upon the footsteps of the fugitives, the Indians hewed them down as they ran, scalping and hacking the bodies of their victims in the most barbarous manner.

The cool forethought and heroism of Captain Bullet, at length put a stop to the sanguinary massacre. Sending back under a slender convoy the strongest horses, with the most valuable part of the baggage, he formed a breastwork of the remainder, as a cover for his troops, and a rallying point for the fugitives. By keeping up a close and well directed fire, he was enabled to check for some time the advance of the pursuers. Finding, from the rapidly increasing strength of the savages, that he was in danger of being speedily overpowered, he resorted to a manœuvre, which can only be justified by the extremity of his peril, and his knowledge of the treacherous character of those with whom he had to deal. Ordering his troops to reverse their arms, as a signal of surrender, he led them slowly, in this manner, toward the expectant savages, already grasping their tomahawks to begin the carnage anew. At a distance of only eight yards from the enemy, he suddenly halted his men, poured a close and destructive volley into the congregated groups, and instantly followed it by a furious charge with fixed bayonets. Struck with astonishment and terror, the Indians, imagining the whole army was at hand, took the woods, and did not cease their flight until they found themselves once more under the protection of the French regulars. Prudently refraining from pursuit, Bullet fell back upon the main body of the army at Loyal Hanna; collecting as he retreated the wounded and terrified soldiers, whom he found scattered along his line of march, exhausted from want of food, and haunted by incessant fears of the savages. In this fatal action, nearly three hundred men were either killed or taken prisoners. The first Virginia regiment lost six officers, and sixty-two privates.

The gallantry of the provincials in the previous battle, in the subsequent repulse of the victorious savages, and in their masterly retreat, was the theme of universal praise.

It was not until the 8th of November, that General Forbes was able to join Bouquet with the main army and heavy baggage. The difficulties in opening the new route were both serious and discouraging. The army, weary of repeated delays, and weakened by sickness and desertion, began to exhibit symptoms of discontent. Fifty miles of unbroken forest yet lay between the camp at Loyal Hanna and Fort Duquesne.

As the winter was close at hand, a council of war advised the abandonment of the enterprise until the opening of spring; but before this decision was acted upon, three prisoners, accidentally captured, reported the enemy as enfeebled by the failure of their usual supplies from the north, and by the desertion of their Indian allies.

An advance was immediately resolved upon. Washington, at his own request, was placed in command of the troops thrown forward to prepare the way for the main army. Leaving their baggage and artillery at Loyal Hanna, the troops partook of the newly revived ardour of their officers, and in despite of the numerous obstacles by which their march was delayed, reached Fort Duquesne on the 20th of November, 1758; but the enemy had already disappeared. The day previous to the arrival of the army under Forbes, they had set fire to the works, and retreated down the Ohio in boats. The ruined walls were speedily renewed, and the long dreaded Fort Duquesne received the name of Fort Pitt, in honour of the English minister. After garrisoning the post with two hundred men, selected from the Virginia regiment, Forbes, whose health was daily becoming more infirm, returned with the main army to Philadelphia, where he died a few weeks after his arrival.

The possession of Fort Pitt soon proved of incalculable advantage to the provinces of Virginia, Maryland, and Pennsylvania. No longer stimulated to hostilities by the French, and awed by the successes of the British arms at the north, the Indian tribes were effectually controlled, and in a little while the fugitive settlers were enabled to return to the frontiers, and occupy their homes in peace.

At the north the war was prosecuted with signal vigour and success. Louisburg had fallen before the combined forces of Abercrombie and Boscawen, and Fort Frontenac had surrendered to a strong detachment of provincials under Broadstreet.

The campaign of 1759 was marked by still greater triumphs. Fort Niagara was captured by the levies under Prideaux and Johnson. During the same month the regulars, under Amherst, took possession of the important fortresses of Crown Point and Ticonderoga, and the conquest of all the French possessions in Canada was completed, on the eighteenth of September, by the surrender of Quebec to the forces commanded by the gallant and lamented Wolfe.

But while the loss of her North American territories restored peace to the British provinces, it was not until 1762 that France consented to the humiliating concessions which were extorted from her by the treaty of Fontainbleau. By this treaty she ceded to Great Britain the whole of Canada, Cape Breton, the islands in the gulf and river of St. Lawrence, part of Louisiana east of the Mississippi River, and her possessions in the West Indies.

The bitterness of feeling engendered by this loss of territory, displayed itself a few years later, in prompting her to retaliate upon Great Britain, by rendering assistance to the colonists in their struggle for independence.

CHAPTER XXII.

English financial embarrassment—Proposition to tax the colonies—Passage of the stamp act—Its reception in America—Patrick Henry—His birth and education—Studies law—His first speech in the "parson's cause"—Its effect upon his auditors—Elected a member of the assembly—Offers his celebrated resolutions—The effect of their adoption—Congress at Philadelphia—Solemn declaration of rights—Repeal of the stamp act—Townshend's new bill—Passed by the Imperial parliament—Resistance of the Americans—Death of Fauquier—Session of 1768—Resolutions of the assembly—Dissolved by the arrival of Lord Bottetourt as governor-in-chief—Session of 1769—Dissolution of the assembly—Non-importation agreement—Progress of resistance—Repeal of all duties except that on tea—Agitation still continues—Death of Lord Bottetourt—His character—The assembly order a statue to be erected to his memory.

THE immense accession of territory acquired by the treaty of Fontainbleau, was soon discovered to be but a poor compensation for the alarming financial embarrassments into which England became plunged by the enormous expenses of the war. The energy infused by Pitt into her councils, the indomitable bravery of her regular troops, and the acknowledged prowess of her provincial levies, had raised her to the enviable position of the greatest power in Europe. But the honour of this supremacy had been dearly bought. Four prolonged wars, within three quarters of a century, had increased her national debt to nearly seven hundred millions of dollars, and had reduced, by excessive taxation, her own immediate subjects to the verge of bankruptcy. A part of these difficulties were undoubtedly occasioned by the large sums of money required to protect the British American provinces from the aggressions of the French. In order to relieve the people of England from so onerous a burden in future, it was thought advisable to draw a revenue from the colonies sufficient to cover the charge of their defence. Hitherto, the colonial assemblies had been permitted to exercise their own discretion in granting or withholding military contributions. Jealous of their independence, and tenacious of a privilege they had so long enjoyed, they denied the authority of the imperial parliament to tax them without their own consent. The power to regulate the colonial trade with foreign countries, although it had been exercised by the officers of the crown for several generations, had always been submitted to with reluctance, and was daily growing more unpopular. Even the charges for the support of a post office, although the latter was an acknowledged benefit, had not been consented to without opposition. Having thus, by the imposition of duties for the regulation of trade, opened the way for more serious exactions, the English government finally resolved to assert its rights to levy taxes for revenue.

In 1763, Lord Granville gave notice of his intention to bring in a bill imposing duty on stamps, avowedly for the purpose of raising a revenue from the provinces. At the next session of parliament, a resolution, affirming the right to tax the colonies, passed the House of Commons without a division. Petitions and remonstrances soon after flowed in from all parts of America. Notwithstanding the intense excitement which the ministry were conscious of having created, the bill was brought forward, and on the 22d of March, 1765, the Stamp Act was finally imposed.

No sooner did its passage become known in America, than Virginia and Massachusetts took the lead in opposition to its enforcement. The assembly of Virginia was in session when the tidings arrived. Among the newly elected burgesses was Patrick Henry, a young lawyer, then just rising into celebrity for an eloquence seldom equalled, and never excelled. Of the knowledge derived from a scholastic education, he possessed but little. He had been taught Latin by his father, and had attained to some proficiency in mathematics, but the confinement of study was his aversion. He better loved to wander with his gun across his shoulder through the intricate mazes of the forest; or to recline by the brook-side beneath the shade of some far-spreading tree, where, lulled into a dreamy mood by the sound of rippling waters, he could indulge for hours together in his own thick coming fancies. When he grew to manhood he became by turns a merchant and a farmer. Equally unsuccessful in both occupations, he determined to study law. After a course of reading which his poverty limited to six weeks, he obtained, in the twenty-fourth year of his age, a license to practice. Utterly ignorant at first of the simplest business of his profession, the three succeeding years were passed in the greatest pecuniary distress. But the leisure which the absence of clients imposed was not wholly unimproved. He divided his time between his favourite sports, the reading of books upon ancient and modern history, and a close study of the ancient Virginia charters. At length, an opportunity occurred for the display of those extraordinary powers, which have handed his name to posterity as the greatest natural orator the world has ever known.

It was the celebrated "Parsons' cause." The salary of the Episcopal ministers in Virginia had been fixed by law at sixteen thousand pounds of tobacco, the value of which long usage had established at sixteen shillings and eight pence a hundred weight. The issue of paper money, and the subsequent rage for speculation, having raised the price of that staple to fifty shillings a hundred weight, laws were passed in 1755 and 1758, authorizing the payment of all tobacco debts in money, at the old rate of sixteen shillings and eight pence. These laws were contested by the clergy, who claimed the right to receive their salary in tobacco, according to the terms of the original statute, or an amount in money equivalent to the increased price of the staple. A previous decision of the court in favour of the claimants, had left nothing undetermined but the amount of damages, the standard of which had been established by the law of 1748. The plaintiff in the present case was Henry's own uncle. Naturally awkward in his deportment, and confused by the presence of so many learned men, and by the multitude of anxious listeners with which the court-house was thronged, Henry faltered so much in his exordium, that his father, who occupied the chair as presiding magistrate, sank back in his seat, covered with shame and mortification. The immense crowd which had assembled within and without the court-house, painfully impressed with the incapacity of their chosen champion, hung their heads in despondency; while the clergy, some twenty of whom were present, glanced at each other with a covert expression of anticipated triumph.

But a wonderful change of feeling was now about to take place. The first few, feeble, and broken sentences, were succeeded by others better connected, and full of pith and meaning. As he gained confidence, the young rustic lawyer disappeared, and in his place stood the impassioned orator, holding the multitude in thrall by the grandeur of his expression, the intense fire which shone in his eyes, the grace of his action, the graphic force of his imagery, and the almost magical charm of a voice which now stirred all hearts, like the blast of a war-bugle, and now soothed them to quietude, as by the tender music of a lute.

The cause was gained; under the bewildering influence of an eloquence almost miraculous, the jury, forgetting alike the clear provisions of the law, and the conceded right of the plaintiff, returned a verdict of one penny damages.

Henry rose rapidly in popularity. The following year he amazed a committee of the house of burgesses, by a brilliant display of his peculiar powers, on a question involving the right of suffrage. In 1765, he was elected to the assembly. He had taken his seat but a few days, when tidings reached Virginia that the Stamp Act had passed. As a member of a body composed principally of the aristocracy of the province, a stranger to most of the burgesses, and entirely unacquainted with the forms of the house, Henry waited for some time the action of older and more experienced men. But finding, as the period approached when the law was to go into operation, that all shrank from grappling with a question involving issues of so momentous a character, he tore from an old law-book a blank leaf, on which he wrote a series of resolutions, claiming for the people of Virginia all the privileges of British subjects; asserting the exclusive right of the assembly to impose taxes upon the people of the colony; and declaring any attempt to vest that authority elsewhere, as inconsistent with the ancient charter of Virginia, and subversive of British, as well as of American freedom. Resolutions so bold and spirited alarmed the fears of those who styled themselves the friends of the government, and gave rise to violent debates.

Henry at once took his place at the head of the liberals. Ardent and uncompromising, he poured forth his magnificent philippics, startling his aristocratic antagonists by the power of his language, the fiery impetuosity of his gestures, and the singular aptness of his comparisons. Warming with his theme, he blanched the cheeks of his auditors, by exclaiming: "Cæsar had his

Brutus; Charles the First his Cromwell; and George the Third"—"Treason! treason!" exclaimed the speaker. "Treason! treason!" echoed other burgesses. Henry turned his fine eyes, blazing with light, from one opponent to another, and then added: "and George the Third may profit by their example. If that be treason, make the most of it." After a warm contest, the resolutions passed by a small majority. The next day the governor dissolved the assembly.

The news spread with astonishing celerity throughout the whole length and breadth of America. Similar resolutions were offered and carried in the other provinces, and the principle of resistance to taxation without representation, was universally established and recognised. Acting upon the recommendation of Massachusetts, deputies from nine provinces met in congress at Philadelphia, and agreed upon a solemn declaration of rights. Petitions and memorials to the King of England and both houses of Parliament were also unanimously adopted, in which the invasion of ancient privileges, and the frequent violations of existing compacts, were complained of in language combining the tenderness of affectionate respect, with the firmness arising from a consciousness of injury. For a whole year the contest continued; but the pertinacity of the British ministry was not equal to the unyielding resolution with which the scheme of imperial taxation was opposed. The stamps were every where refused. Pitt, Camden, Barre, Burke, and Conway openly justified the Americans in their resistance. Finding the obnoxious act utterly ineffective for all practical purposes, it was repealed by Parliament at the session of 1766.

The joy of the provincials was, however, but of short duration. Their expressions of loyalty and gratitude had scarcely subsided, before Townsend, the new chancellor of the exchequer, sheltering himself behind the admitted right of Parliament to regulate commerce, framed a bill imposing certain duties on tea, paper, glass, and painters' colours.

On the second of July, 1767, the act was passed. Justly indignant at this new and more insidious attempt to encroach upon their liberties, the Americans entered at once upon a spirited resistance. They contended, that when designed for purposes of revenue, there was no difference in principle between direct and indirect taxation.

Before the passage of the act was known in Virginia the death of Lieutenant-governor Fauquier had again placed John Blair, president of the council, at the head of the government.

Difficulties having arisen between the people of the frontiers and the western Indians, the as sembly was convened a month earlier than usual. It met on the last of March, 1768. After adopting such measures as were best calculated to quiet the border agitation, the burgesses proceeded to consider the late acts of Parliament, and passed a series of spirited resolutions, in which they boldly asserted, "that no power on earth has a right to impose taxes on the people without their own consent." While still in session, Lord Bottetourt, the new governor-in-chief, arrived, and a dissolution immediately took place. As this was the usual course of procedure in such cases, it created no dissatisfaction.

In accordance with a previous summons to that effect, a new assembly convened in May, 1769; and, after listening respectfully to a conciliatory speech from the governor, entered upon an animated discussion of grievances. The Parliament of December, 1768, having authorized the governor of Massachusetts to be instructed to send to England for trial all persons charged with treasonable offences, the assembly of Virginia anticipated the reception of similar orders by the adoption of several resolutions, in which they claimed the sole power to impose taxes, asserted their right to petition the crown for relief, either singly or in conjunction with other colonies, and denounced the transmission beyond sea for trial, of any persons suspected of treason or of any other crime whatsoever, as a violation of privilege, and an illegal departure from a fixed and known course of proceeding. These resolutions were ordered to be sent, without delay, to the speakers of the several houses of assembly on the continent, and disdaining any longer to appeal to an unfriendly Parliament, the burgesses agreed upon an address, to be presented by their colonial agent to the king in person. Although sincerely sympathizing with the colonists in their troubles, the governor, holding his office from the crown, could not suffer resolutions of so dangerous a character to pass without a pointed rebuke.

The following morning he dissolved the assembly. Undeterred by this censure, the members adjourned to a private dwelling, and solemnly pledged themselves to import no articles from England, or any part of Europe, except an enumerated few, which were of absolute and primary necessity. Among the burgesses by whom this non-importation agreement was signed, were George Washington, Patrick Henry, and Thomas Jefferson; the latter, a young lawyer newly elected from the county of Albemarle, where he possessed a handsome patrimonial estate.

Animated by the imposing example of Virginia, such of the other colonies as had previously hesitated to commit themselves to measures so decided, now adopted resolutions of a similar character.

Alarmed at the fearful progress of a resistance which they themselves had provoked, the British ministry, at length, reluctantly retraced their steps, and in April, 1770, the obnoxious duties were repealed, with the exception of three pence a pound on tea. To render the latter acceptable to the Americans, a drawback of one shilling a pound was allowed on all tea exported to the colonies, so that they were, apparently, benefited by the change to the extent of nine pence a pound.

But the original ground of contest still remained. The right to tax one article involved the right to tax all; and though a relaxation of the non-importation agreement took place as soon as the duties on the other commodities were removed, the colonists determined to allow no tea to be landed in America, until the impost on that also was rescinded.

The death of their amiable and upright governor, Lord Bottetourt, during the fall of this year, was a source of sincere regret to the people of Virginia. Engaging in his address, prompt in his attention to business, and of incorruptible integrity, he yet more closely endeared himself to all, by the deep interest which he showed for the welfare of the province, and by the frank, bold, and energetic manner in which he defended those over whom he presided from the aspersions of their enemies. More than once he warned the British government of the danger that was likely to ensue from persisting in a course of policy that would inevitably prove as injurious to the true interests of England, as it was unjust to her colonies.

Acting under his instructions from abroad, he had, from time to time, given assurances to his council and the house of burgesses, which the ministry never intended to fulfil. Justly indignant at a deception, to which he had been made a party, the high spirited nobleman demanded his recall; declaring, at the same time, his determination never to suffer himself to be constituted the oppressor of an innocent and virtuous people.

Profoundly penetrated by the remembrance of his many virtues, the members of the house of burgesses ordered a fine marble statue, which still stands in the town of Williamsburg, to be erected to his memory.

CHAPTER XXIII.

Dunmore appointed governor—Arrival of Foy—Meeting of the assembly—Rebuke of Dunmore—His tart reply—Committee of correspondence organized—A continental Congress suggested—Journey of Dunmore to the Ohio—Appoints Conolly Indian agent—His designs unfolded—Troubles with Pennsylvania—Action of the Virginia council—Cargoes of tea sent to the colonies—Proceedings in consequence—Destruction of tea at Boston—Its port closed—Action of Virginia—The Continental Congress—Indian war on the frontier—An army raised—March of Dunmore—Colonel Lewis encamps at Point Pleasant—Battle of Point Pleasant—Suspicious conduct of Dunmore—Negotiations for peace—Speech of Logan—Approaching crisis—Battle of Lexington—Dunmore conveys the powder from the magazine at Williamsburg—Henry marches upon the capital—An assembly convened—Flight of Dunmore.

By the death of the lamented Bottetourt, the duties of governor devolved upon William Nelson, president of the council, until the arrival of Lord Dunmore in 1772. The quartering of troops in Boston, the riots in that city during the spring of 1770, and the obstinate persistence of the British ministry in retaining the duty on tea, all tended to increase the agitation of the public mind. Slight events became causes of grave suspicion; and while every one felt that a crisis was rapidly approaching, none knew upon which province the blow was first to fall. The delay of Dunmore, in New York, for several months after his appointment, was by no means favourable to his reputation in Virginia. The resignation by Captain Foy of his office as Governor of New Hampshire, for the purpose of accepting the inferior post of private secretary to Dunmore, was regarded by many as originating in some latent purpose. Foy had obtained a brilliant military reputation by his conduct at the battle of Minden; and it was supposed, not without plausibility, that the British ministry intended to employ his talents in carrying out those measures of coercion which had already been devised. To provide an adequate salary for his distinguished secretary, Dunmore had directed that he should receive a fixed sum of five hundred pounds a year, besides the lucrative emoluments arising from a list of fees established expressly for his benefit. This assumption of an authority vested in the assembly alone, received, at the first meeting of that body, a prompt rebuke; and Dunmore, conscious of the impolicy of creating an open rupture with the indignant burgesses upon a question of so little moment when compared with the one at issue between the provinces and the mother country, consented to annul the new list of fees, and sought by his courtesy and condescension to efface the unfavourable impression his conduct had created. For a brief period harmony was apparently restored, but before the assembly again met, in 1773, a forgery of colonial paper money to an alarming extent, while stimulating the governor to bring the supposed offenders to justice, had led him to overstep the strict limits of the law. Conscious that one uncensured illegal act might afford a pretext for others, the assembly resolved upon an address to Dunmore, in which they stated, that as a doubtful construction, and various execution of the criminal code, would greatly endanger the safety of the innocent, they trusted that the proceedings in the case under notice might not be adduced in future as a precedent. Stung by the rebuke, Dunmore answered tartly, "In apprehending and bringing to justice the forgers of your paper currency, I little imagined, when I was endeavouring to punish the guilty, that my conduct could by any means be thought to endanger the safety of the innocent." This display of acerbity had no effect upon men who were sustained by the consciousness of having performed a duty which they owed to their constituents.

After having thus zealously defended the privileges of the subject, the burgesses proceeded to organize a committee of correspondence, for the purpose of keeping up a frequent communication with the other colonies, and of obtaining the earliest intelligence from abroad. The subsequent movements of Dunmore were also subjected to the closest scrutiny.

During the summer he proceeded on a pleasure excursion to the back settlements. He remained sometime at Pittsburg, examining the nature of the country, conciliating the inhabitants, and holding frequent interviews of a private nature with one Conolly, whom he had appointed Indian agent. This man, able and unscrupulous, was known to possess considerable influence, not only over the surrounding tribes of savages, but also with the hardy and unsuspicious borderers. The objects of Dunmore's journey soon became apparent. It was to create a territorial dispute between Virginia and Pennsylvania, and thus weaken the bond of union existing between the two provinces; or failing in that, to divert the attention of Virginia from the designs of the British government by provoking an Indian war. He had scarcely set out on his return, before Conolly commenced the formation of settlements in Pennsylvania, under patents granted by Dunmore. These encroachments were immediately resisted, Conolly was seized and imprisoned by the officers of Pennsylvania, and the settlers secured and punished as outlaws. Dunmore instantly issued a proclamation, which was well calculated, by its violent and haughty tone, to increase the excitement already existing. Fortunately his scheme was foiled by the sagacity and moderation of his council, who firmly rejecting all violent measures, agreed to settle the controversy by arbitration.

In the mean while, the general adoption of the

non-importation agreement having had the effect of virtually annulling the tax upon tea, the British government endeavoured to force its introduction into the colonies by offering the East India Company a drawback equal to the amount of duty. As the tax was by this means rendered merely nominal, the hope was indulged that resistance would cease, and the proposition was accepted by the company. But as the principle involved remained the same as ever, the people would not yield.

At Charleston, the tea was allowed to be stored, but its sale was expressly prohibited. The cargoes intended for Philadelphia and New York, were sent back at once to England. At Boston, the popular indignation displayed itself far more violently. On the evening of the 16th of December, 1773, three ships, containing tea, were boarded by an organized party, disguised as Indians, who forcibly broke open the chests containing the obnoxious commodity, and emptied their contents into the water. This bold act was no sooner known in England, than a bill was passed by Parliament, closing the port of Boston, and removing the seat of government to Salem.

The assembly of Virginia was in session when a rough draft of the bill reached Williamsburg. All other business was at once thrown aside. An order was passed forthwith, protesting against the conduct of the ministry as subversive of

American freedom, and setting apart that day week—the 1st of June, 1774—for the purpose of fasting, humiliation, and prayer. To put a stop to proceedings so alarming, Dunmore summoned the members to the council chamber, and dissolved the assembly.

On the following day, the whole of the delegates repaired, by agreement, to the Raleigh tavern, where, after drawing up an address to the American people, they authorized a correspondence to be opened with the several colonial committees, suggesting the expediency of appointing delegates to meet in a general Congress. The proposal everywhere met with a favourable response. On the 1st of August, 1774, a convention was held at Williamsburg, which, after adopting, in a more stringent form, the old non-importation agreement, appointed seven delegates to the proposed Congress. Prominent among those chosen, were Randolph, Washington, Henry, and Jefferson.

The Continental Congress met at Philadelphia on the 4th of September following. It consisted of fifty-three delegates, the leading men of twelve provinces. Of this select assembly, Peyton Randolph was chosen president.

But while the patriotism of Virginia was being thus honoured by her sister provinces, she was suffering all the horrors of an Indian war upon her frontiers. Preluded by a series of atrocious murders, it suddenly burst in full fury upon the defenceless inhabitants. The parties of border militia which had assembled to check the progress of the enemy, were swept away, and such settlers as did not seek safety in flight, were either barbarously massacred, or hurried into captivity.

No longer dreading the effects of French skill, superadded to Indian ferocity, large numbers of volunteers immediately took the field. An army of twenty-seven hundred men was speedily raised. Dunmore, to whom, by means of his agent Conolly, the war has been attributed, placed himself at the head of a division of fifteen hundred men, and marched against the Shawanese towns on the Scioto. The remaining division under Colonel Andrew Lewis, proceeded to Point Pleasant, at the mouth of the great Kanawha.

As a junction was to have been made at this place with the troops under Dunmore, Lewis halted his men and encamped until the first division should arrive. On the 9th of October, orders were received from the governor for the troops to cross the Ohio and join him at, or near, the Shawanese towns. Early the next morning, while the men were actively engaged in preparing for their march, several wounded scouts came into camp with intelligence that the Indians had been discovered in great force at a distance of less than a mile from the point. The main body of the army was immediately ordered out under Colonels Charles Lewis, and Fleming. The advance, under Lewis, had not proceeded more than four hundred yards before it was assaulted by the Indians, and the action commenced. At the first fire Colonel Lewis fell mortally wounded. Fleming being disabled soon after, the men fell back in some confusion toward the camp, but were speedily rallied under cover of a reinforcement commanded by Colonel Field. The engagement then became general, and was continued, with unabated fury, from sunrise until near the close of evening. A skilful manœuvre, executed under the orders of Colonel Andrew Lewis, at length decided the victory in favour of the Americans. Three companies, commanded by Shelby, Matthews, and Stuart, were directed to proceed secretly up the Kanawha, turn the position of the enemy, and suddenly fall upon their rear. This movement was successfully accomplished. Alarmed at being placed unexpectedly between two fires, the Indians were thrown into disorder, and about sunset commenced a precipitate retreat across the Ohio to their towns on the Scioto. In this hard fought battle the Virginians sustained a loss in killed and wounded of two hundred and fifteen.

As soon as the dead were buried, and arrangements made for the comfort of the wounded, Lewis pressed forward to form a junction with

Dunmore. While he was on his march, he was met by an express bearing orders for the troops to return at once to Point Pleasant. Suspicious of the motives by which the governor was actuated, Lewis continued to advance, until he came in sight of one of the Indian towns, where he encountered Dunmore in person, who informed him that he had already consented to enter upon negotiations for a peace.

At the treaty, which was concluded soon after, Logan, one of the principal chiefs, was not present. To avoid, however, any misconstruction of his motives, he sent, by General Gibson, the following speech to Lord Dunmore: "I appeal to any white man to say, if ever he entered Logan's cabin hungry, and he gave him not meat; if ever he came cold and naked, and he clothed him not. During the course of the last long and bloody war, Logan remained idle in his cabin, an advocate for peace. Such was my love for the whites, that my countrymen pointed, as they passed, and said, 'Logan is the friend of the white man.' I had even thought to have lived with you, but for the injuries of one man. Colonel Cresap, the last spring, in cold blood, and unprovoked, murdered all the relations of Logan, not even sparing my women and children. There run not a drop of my blood in the veins of any living creature. This called on me for revenge. I have sought it: I have killed many: I have fully glutted my vengeance. For my country I rejoice at the beams of peace. But do not harbour a thought that mine is the joy of fear. Logan never felt fear. He will not turn on his heel to save his life. Who is there to mourn for Logan! Not one."

The war was closed upon the frontier; but a sterner, grander, and more prolonged contest was speedily approaching. Resolutions, addresses, and resistance, both passive and forcible, had fully aroused the spirit of the American colonies, and prepared them for the bloodier struggle which was to follow. The common cause, at first imperfectly embraced, because imperfectly understood, was now sustained by an unanimity of action, as forcible as it was imposing.

In the early part of 1775, the various provincial governors received instructions from England, to check the disposition to rebellion in the colonies, by seizing upon all depots of arms and ammunition. Gage, of Massachusetts, was the first to undertake the fulfilment of this order, by an attempt to capture some cannon and military stores collected at Concord, a small town some twenty miles from Boston. Eight hundred troops were detached on this service, and on the nineteenth of April, at sunrise, reached Lexington, where, for the first time, they came into collision with a body of continental militia. The regulars were at first successful, but were subsequently compelled to retreat to Boston, with a loss in killed and wounded of three hundred men.

On the 22d of April, two days only after the battle of Lexington, Dunmore secretly removed the gunpowder from the magazine at Williamsburg, to an armed vessel lying off York Town. This act was no sooner discovered than the volunteers of Williamsburg assembled in arms, with the avowed purpose of seizing the person of the governor.

Restrained with difficulty from the immediate execution of their threat, they despatched a deputation to the governor, demanding a restitution of the powder. His reply was courteous, but evasive. In the midst of the excitement, news arrived of the fight at Lexington. The tidings spread like wild-fire throughout the province. Fifteen hundred men collected at Fredericksburg from the upper country, prepared to march at a moment's warning to the defence of the capital, which Dunmore had threatened to lay in ashes at the first signal of insurrection. By the influence of Randolph, and other patriotic gentlemen, this large force was prevailed upon to abstain from active hostilities until the continental congress should decide upon the proper course to be pursued. Firm in his belief that the time for action had arrived, Patrick Henry alone refused to consent to any proposition involving delay. Placing himself at the head of his own company of volunteers from Hanover county, he marched at once upon Williamsburg. By the time he had reached Doncastle's ordinary, sixteen miles from the seat of government, his force had swelled to five hundred men. As he approached the city he was met by deputies from Williamsburg, accompanied by Corbin, the king's receiver, who consented to give bills for the value of the powder taken away. The particular cause of quarrel being thus removed, Henry returned to Hanover county, and on the 4th of May disbanded his followers.

While the deputies were treating with Henry, Dunmore sent his family on board the Fowey man-of-war, and after fortifying his palace, garrisoned it, in addition to his own armed servants, and the Shawanese hostages, with a party of marines which he had ordered to his assistance from one of the ships in the river.

These preparations for resistance, joined to the threat made by Captain Montague, that if his detachment met with any interruption, he would open a fire upon the town of York, brought on a renewal of the excitement. A proclamation by Dunmore declaring Henry and his followers guilty of rebellion, added fuel to the flame.

Stimulated to increased activity, meetings were held in every county, and volunteers pledged themselves to be in readiness to march wherever their services might be required. In this threatening aspect of affairs, Dunmore, fearing to trust himself beyond the walls of his palace, called his council together and asked their advice. They suggested that the marines should be dismissed, and an assembly convened. The governor reluctantly consented. A brief period of quiet succeeded, but confidence was not restored. It was rumoured abroad that a scheme was being arranged for the seizure of the newly-elected deputies, who were openly warned to come prepared. Undeterred by the mysterious danger with which they were menaced, the delegates fearlessly set out for the capital. Those from distant counties entered Williamsburg dressed in their hunting shirts, and bearing their rifles. Nearly all who attended were armed. They had scarcely reached the city before an attempt was made to break open the magazine. In the act of entering it, a spring gun exploded, wounding one of the persons engaged in the affair. An alarming riot followed, and Dunmore, fearful for his personal safety, fled secretly by night, and took refuge on board the Fowey.

CHAPTER XXIV.

Adjournment of the Virginia Assembly—Continental Congress —Washington appointed commander-in-chief—Battle of Bunker's Hill—Movements of Dunmore—Battle at Great Bridge—Norfolk evacuated—Bombarded and burned—Meeting of the Assembly—New constitution adopted—Declaration of Independence—Retreat of Dunmore—War at the north—Disastrous expedition against Quebec—Retreat of Washington across the Jerseys—Battles of Trenton and Princeton—Campaign of 1777—March of Burgoyne from Canada—Capture of Ticonderoga—Surrender of Burgoyne—Movements of Howe—Battles of Brandywine and Germantown—Washington retires to Valley Forge—Treaty of alliance with France—Howe evacuates Philadelphia—Clinton retreats across the Jerseys—Battle of Monmouth—Arrival of a French fleet off the Capes—An attack upon Newport projected—Its failure—Invasion of the southern states—Virginia plundered by General Matthews.

The flight of the governor was no sooner discovered, than the council and assembly agreed upon a joint address, entreating him to return to the palace, and offering to concur in any measure that might be considered necessary for his personal security. On his refusal to do so, the assembly declared his office vacant, and appointed the president of the council in his place. They adjourned themselves soon after, having first agreed to meet in convention at Richmond, for the purpose of organizing a provisional government, and arranging a plan of defence. While the Virginia assembly were thus endeavouring to induce Dunmore to return to Williamsburg and resume the duties of his office, the continental congress, then in session at Philadelphia, after declaring that hostilities with Great Britain had commenced, had appointed George Washington commander-in-chief of the continental army. This appointment was made on the 15th of June, 1775.

On the 17th, was fought the battle of Bunker's Hill. Four days afterward, Washington left Philadelphia to assume command of the troops, then stationed at Cambridge.

On the 17th of July, according to previous agreement, the Virginia convention met, entrusted the executive authority to a committee of safety, and ordered the immediate enlistment of two regiments of Minute Men. The royal government of Virginia was at an end.

Dunmore, having with him several armed vessels and two companies of regulars, still hovered about Old Point Comfort, and threatened the lower counties. Hoping to create a diversion in his favour west of the mountains, he had sent to his former agent Conolly, the commission of a lieutenant-colonel; but his project failed of success by the arrest of Conolly in Maryland, while returning from a visit to General Gage at Boston.

Landing at Norfolk, then just rising into a town of some commercial importance, Dunmore seized a printing press, and on the 17th November, issued a proclamation, declaring martial law, and offering freedom to all slaves belonging to rebels who would join the royal standard. A large number of negroes and tories responded to the call. With this mixed force he commenced offensive operations. Marching to Kempsville, in Princess Anne county, he destroyed some arms collected there, and took several prisoners, among whom was Captain Mathews, of the Minute Men. Having threatened the inhabitants of Hampton with an attack, the committee of safety sent Colonel Woodford with a hundred riflemen to assist in defending the place. Before he could arrive, six tenders, filled with men, entered Hampton Creek, and endeavoured to effect a landing, for the purpose of burning and plundering the town; but as the enemy approached the shore in boats, they were driven back by a party of concealed riflemen. Night set in; and, in the mean time, the reinforcement under Woodford arrived. In the morning a second attempt to land was resisted with even greater success than the former; the enemy then withdrew to Norfolk.

Desirous of striking a decisive blow, the committee of safety determined to force Dunmore to evacuate Norfolk. Woodford's second Virginia regiment and the Culpepper battalion were ordered upon this service. At Great Bridge, a few miles from Norfolk, the enemy occupied a stockade fort, which, being furnished with artillery, and strongly garrisoned, effectually protected the approach to the city. Woodford threw up a breastwork at the end of the causeway, and waited for the arrival of reinforcements. Deceived by a stratagem as to the number of the provincials, Captain Fordyce, at the head of three hundred and fifty regulars, tories, and negroes, sallied out from the fort on the morning of the ninth of December, 1775, to attack Woodford in his entrenchments. While advancing along the causeway, Fordyce fell mortally wounded, and his troops, after having sustained a loss of nearly one-third of their whole number, in an action which lasted only thirty minutes, gave way and retreated precipitately to the fort. Alarmed at this unexpected defeat, Dunmore hastily spiked his artillery, abandoned his works, and embarked with the remainder of his army on board the vessels in the harbour. Five days after the skirmish at Great Bridge, the Virginians, reinforced by the North Carolina militia under Colonel Robert Howe, took possession of Norfolk, and opened a fire upon the British ships. In retaliation for this rash provocation, and for the rough treatment which certain royalists had experienced from the conquerors, Dunmore, strengthened by the arrival of the frigate Liverpool, bombarded the town on the first of January, 1776, and, landing a party of marines and seamen under cover of the cannonade, set fire to it in several places.

Of a thousand houses, nearly nine hundred were consumed. The remainder were destroyed soon after by order of the committee of safety.

During the whole of the summer following, Dunmore, sailing up the various rivers of eastern Virginia, carried on a series of petty predatory incursions, by which the loyalists sustained great losses. Plantations were ravaged, houses were burned, and nearly a thousand slaves abducted from their masters. At length, although moving with celerity from point to point, and retreating to his boats whenever menaced with a serious attack, he found himself so continually harassed by armed parties of volunteers and militia, that he was constrained to withdraw his motley force, and retire to St. Augustine with the plunder he had accumulated.

The general assembly of Virginia met at Williamsburg on the 6th of May, and after appointing Edmund Pendleton president, and John Tazewell clerk, proceeded to the business before them. On the 15th of the month it was unanimously agreed upon to instruct the Virginia delegation to the continental congress, then in session at Philadelphia, to propose in that body a formal declaration of independence, and the absolution of the United Colonies from all allegiance to Great Britain. A committee was also appointed to prepare a declaration of rights, and a plan of government suitable to the new condition of the province. On the 29th the constitution, framed by George Mason, with a preamble sent by Jefferson from Philadelphia, was unanimously adopted. Patrick Henry received the appointment of governor. On the 5th of July the assembly adjourned. At Philadelphia, the day previous, the declaration of Independence as drawn up by Jefferson was passed by Congress. It was proclaimed at Williamsburg on the 25th of the same month amid the firing of cannon, and the exulting shouts of the assembled people.

The assembly again met on the 7th of October, 1776, and appointed a committee to revise the state laws. By the strenuous efforts of Jefferson and Mason, an act was passed at this session, by which dissenters were relieved from the disabilities under which they had laboured previously, and all forms of religion placed upon an equal footing.

From the retreat of Dunmore, until the summer of 1779, the territory of Virginia was happily exempted from that fearful condition of things which always accompanies the march of hostile armies. At the north, in the mean time, the forces sent over by Great Britain had been kept constantly engaged. The campaign of 1776 opened disastrously for the American cause. The army ordered to attempt the reduction of Canada had met with a signal defeat before the walls of Quebec, where Montgomery, its heroic leader, fell mortally wounded. The Virginians under Morgan, though fighting bravely in the midst of the storm and darkness, were overpowered by numbers, and compelled to surrender themselves prisoners of war.

During the campaign in Canada, reinforcements from England had raised the royalist army under Howe, to twenty-four thousand men. To oppose this large body of disciplined troops, the American commander-in-chief had a force of about twenty thousand provincials, badly equipped, yielding but little military obedience, and rendered inharmonious by sectional jealousies. The defeat of Putnam on Long Island, compelled Washington to abandon New York to the British and retreat across the Jerseys. With his troops daily diminishing from the expiration of their term of service, from sickness, and desertion, he crossed the Delaware on the 7th of December, at the head of a dispirited army, reduced to three thousand five hundred effective men. One bright gleam, however, shed a lustre over the close of the campaign. With twenty-five hundred picked men, and six pieces of artillery, Washington secretly recrossed the Delaware, on the night of the twenty-fifth of December, 1776, entered Trenton the following morning in the midst of a snow storm, surprised a body of fifteen hundred Hessians stationed at that place, took one thousand of them prisoners of war, and captured their artillery. Astonished at a reverse so little expected, Howe immediately directed Cornwallis to take command of the British force quartered at Princeton, and attack Washington in his camp at Trenton. Finding his position a dangerous one, and retreat difficult in the face of an enemy equal in numbers and far superior in arms and discipline, Washington adopted the bold expedient of occupying the attention of Cornwallis in front, while the provincial army retreated silently from camp and fell upon his rear. The manœuvre succeeded. Near to Princeton three regiments of British regulars on their march to join Cornwallis, were attacked and broken, with the loss of three hundred men taken prisoners. Washington then retired to winter quarters at Morristown, while Cornwallis encamped at New Brunswick.

The British plan of the campaign of 1777 was in many respects similar to that formerly recommended to the French government by De Callier, the design being to separate the New England states from the middle and southern colonies, by opening a communication between New York and Canada. In pursuance of this project, General Burgoyne left Canada with an army of eight thousand men, captured Ticonderoga, dispersed the greater part of the garrison under St. Clair, in their retreat to join Schuyler at Fort Edward, and obtained complete command of lakes George and Champlain. Hitherto Burgoyne had been successful at every point. He was now to experience a series of reverses, which weakened the confidence of his troops, lost him the support of his Indian allies, and finally enveloped him in such a network of difficulties, as constrained him to surrender, on the 17th of October, the whole of his army to General Gates.

In the mean while, the successes of Sir William Howe had created great excitement in the southern and middle states. Sailing up the Chesapeake, he landed at the head of Elk, advanced toward Philadelphia, defeated the American army under Washington at the battles of Brandywine and Germantown, captured the defences on the Delaware, and thereby enabled the British fleet to co-operate with the army. The winter being close at hand, Washington went into quarters at Valley Forge.

The event of greatest importance in the year 1778, was the treaty of defensive alliance signed between France and the American colonies. Fearful of the river Delaware being blockaded by a French fleet, Howe concluded to evacuate Philadelphia, and ordered Clinton to retreat across the Jerseys to New York. On the 19th of June, the British army, twelve thousand strong, crossed the Delaware, and took up its line of march. Washington at once started in pursuit. On the 28th of the same month, the enemy encamped at Monmouth Court House. The following morning

Washington ordered Lee, who commanded the advance, to press forward and commence the action. Lee did so, but in a short time retreated. The troops were rallied by Washington, and a sharp but indecisive engagement ensued. Under cover of the darkness, the British gained the high lands of Nevisink, where they occupied a position secure from attack. From Nevisink, Clinton embarked on board of Howe's fleet, and returned to New York, barely escaping a French squadron of sixteen ships, commanded by the Count D'Estaing, and having on board four thousand French troops, which arrived off the Delaware a few days later.

Desirous of profiting at once by this fortunate event, Washington arranged with the French commander a plan of attack on Newport, Rhode Island, where six thousand of the enemy were garrisoned. General Sullivan, with a strong division of the continental army, was ordered to co-operate with D'Estaing on this service; but the latter being led away by the prospect of bringing the British fleet to an engagement, Sullivan was compelled to abandon his position in front of the town, and retreat hastily across the island to the main land.

Foiled in their efforts to reduce the northern states, the main strength of the British arms was now directed against the south. Georgia was invaded by an army of three thousand five hundred men, commanded by Colonel Campbell, which, forming a junction with the force under Prevost, Governor of Florida, captured Savannah, and speedily overran the whole province.

In the mean while, Clinton, who had succeeded Howe as commander-in-chief of the British forces in America, despatched General Matthews from New York, with twenty-five hundred men, to commence operations against Virginia. The squadron having these troops on board, entered Hampton Roads early in May, and Matthews immediately entered upon a career of plunder and devastation. He took possession of Fort Nelson and the town of Portsmouth, recaptured Norfolk, and destroyed both there, and at Gosport, large quantities of naval and military stores. One hundred and thirty merchant vessels were either captured or burned in the James and Elizabeth rivers, and a frigate and nine smaller ships of war on the stocks at Gosport, were also consumed by fire. Three thousand hogsheads of tobacco formed a portion of the plunder acquired by this expedition, which, though remaining within the limits of the province but a few days, inflicted a damage upon public and private property amounting in the aggregate to two millions of dollars.

CHAPTER XXV.

Clinton embarks for the south—Capture of Charleston—Gates appointed to command the southern continental army.—His defeat at Camden—Leslie sent to Virginia—Greene supersedes Gates—Arnold in Virginia—La Fayette ordered to reinforce Steuben—General Phillips forms a junction with Arnold—Destruction of stores at Yorktown—Petersburg captured—Advance of Cornwallis—Battle of Cowpens—Retreat of Greene—Marches against Rawdon—Cornwallis reaches Petersburg—Expeditions of Simcoe and Tarleton—March of Cornwallis to Portsmouth—Skirmish near Jamestown—The British army concentrated at York and Gloucester—Movements of the allied forces under Washington and Rochambeau—Arrival of the French fleet in the Chesapeake—Yorktown invested—Incidents of the siege—Capitulation of Cornwallis—Negotiations for peace.

The subjugation of Georgia was no sooner completed, than the conquest of the Carolinas was resolved upon. Previous efforts to obtain possession of Charleston having failed, Clinton determined to attempt its reduction in person. Leaving Kniphausen with a strong garrison in New York, he embarked on the 26th of December, 1779, for Savannah, with seven thousand troops. After completing his arrangements at the latter port, he sailed for the harbour of Charleston, which he entered early in April, and proceeded at once to invest the town. On the 14th of April, 1780, two continental regiments stationed at Monk's Corner to keep open the communication with the country north of Broad River, were surprised by Tarleton, and effectually dispersed. Fort Moultrie, threatened by sea and land, surrendered on the 6th of May. In the mean time, Clinton with the main army was pressing forward with great vigour his operations against the town, which was obstinately but unsuccessfully defended by General Lincoln. Finding himself completely surrounded, and with no hope of receiving succour from without, Lincoln at length decided to open negotiations, which resulted in yielding up the city and surrendering its garrison as prisoners of war. Clinton had no sooner acquired possession of Charleston than he spread his forces over the interior of the state. As no opposition was offered, the conquest was speedily completed. Having re-established the royal government, and placed four thousand troops under Cornwallis to maintain his conquest, Clinton returned with the remainder of his forces to New York.

So soon as the capitulation of Lincoln became known to Congress, that body appointed General Gates to command the continental army in the south. Pushing forward at once to overtake the Maryland and Delaware battalions under De Kalb, which had already been detached for service in that quarter, he came up with them at the Deep River, a tributary of the Cape Fear.

Apprehensive of danger, Lord Rawdon, commanding the British advanced posts in South

Carolina, immediately called in his detachments, and concentrated his forces at Camden. Gates marched at once upon that point by the most direct route, gathering strength from Virginia and the Carolinas as he proceeded, until his army was increased to six thousand men. Cornwallis, advised of his approach, hastened from Charleston, formed a junction with Rawdon, and at daybreak on the 6th of August, encountered the southern provincial army in the vicinity of Camden. Gates, rash as he was vain, was utterly defeated, and his troops, routed and pursued, were driven into the swamps and effectually dispersed.

When Clinton heard of the defeat of Gates, supposing that Cornwallis, taking advantage of his victory at Camden, would proceed at once across North Carolina, and attempt to overrun Virginia, he despatched from New York three thousand men, under Colonel Leslie, to the Chesapeake Bay, for the purpose of co-operating with the southern army. But Cornwallis, weakened by the defeat of Ferguson at King's Mountain, and wanting both supplies and reinforcements, was in no condition to advance. Under these circumstances, Leslie's movements were crippled. Landing at Portsmouth, he took possession of a few vessels, plundered some of the plantations on the coast, and then set sail for South Carolina.

In the mean time, Congress had directed General Greene to reorganize and take command of the southern continental army. On his way to the headquarters of Gates at Charlotte, in North Carolina, Greene left Baron Steuben in Virginia to collect recruits, and to assist in defending the state against an expedition, then fitting out at New York.

On the 30th of December, 1780, the traitor Arnold entered the Chesapeake with a fleet of fifty sail, proceeded with nine hundred men to the falls of the James River, and took possession of Richmond without opposition. Sending out a detachment of light horse under Colonel Simcoe to Westham, the latter destroyed the cannon foundry at that place, and such stores as had been hastily removed there from Richmond.

Descending the James River, a few days after, Arnold returned to Portsmouth, plundering and destroying as he went.

The principal part of the Virginia troops having joined the army under Greene, Steuben, finding himself too weak to enter upon offensive operations with the militia which had been hastily collected, was compelled to confine himself to watching the invaders, and restricting their operations. The presence of Arnold in Virginia no sooner became known to Washington, than he formed a project for the capture of the traitor. In pursuance of the plan he had devised, General La Fayette was sent with twelve hundred continentals to reinforce Steuben, and to co-operate with the French squadron, which presently sailed from Newport for the Chesapeake Bay. The scheme, though well devised, was destined to be frustrated. A naval engagement took place off the Capes, between the British and French fleets, in which the latter being worsted, were obliged to return to their former anchorage at Newport.

By the activity of Clinton, a detachment of two thousand men, commanded by Major-general Phillips, was soon after sent to the assistance of Arnold, and the combined forces, supported by the British squadron, speedily renewed the old system of plunder and devastation.

Leaving one thousand men to garrison Portsmouth, Phillips sailed up the James River, and after sending a detachment to destroy the naval stores collected at Yorktown, proceeded to Petersburg, where Steuben with a body of militia, less than one thousand in number, attempted to oppose his progress. After a sharp skirmish, which lasted for about two hours, Steuben retired with his troops to the opposite side of the Appomattox. On the 25th of April, 1781, Phillips entered the town, where he captured and burned, during the following day, four thousand hogsheads of tobacco. Crossing the Appomattox, he marched to Chesterfield Court-house, set fire to the buildings erected at that place for the reception of recruits for the army under Greene, and destroyed the provisions and stores collected there.

In the mean time, Arnold proceeded to Osborne's, where he burned a quantity of tobacco. So soon as Arnold's detachment had formed a junction with the main army, Phillips proceeded to Manchester, a small village opposite to Richmond. The arrival of La Fayette in that vicinity, induced Phillips to re-embark his troops, and fall down the James River; but learning on his way that Cornwallis was advancing into Virginia, he relanded his troops at City Point, and Brandon, and returned hastily to Petersburg, to form a junction with that officer. Suffering under a severe attack of bilious fever, Phillips died a few days after reaching the city. The command of the army then devolved on Arnold.

During the progress of these events in Virginia, Cornwallis had been actively engaged in South Carolina against Greene, and the partizan officers by whom the latter was supported. By the defeat of Tarleton at the "Cowpens," the British lost six hundred men; but reinforced the next day by the troops under Leslie, Cornwallis pressed forward in pursuit of Morgan, hoping to intercept him before he should be able to form a junction with Greene. In this, however, he was not successful. The provincial forces were united, and Greene evinced a determination to defend the passage of the Catawba. The fords being forced by the enemy, Greene, closely pursued, fell back upon the Yadkin. He had scarcely crossed it before the British van came up, but only succeeded in capturing a few wagons.

A sudden rise in the river effectually preventing the enemy from crossing for several days, Greene continued on to Guilford Court-house, from whence he retreated by a forced march into Virginia.

Cornwallis had no sooner returned to the interior of North Carolina, than Greene recrossed the Dan, and threw out skirmishing parties to keep the tories in check on the Haw and Deep Rivers, and to harass detached parties of the enemy's regulars. Being reinforced during the early part of March, 1781, by detachments of continental troops from Virginia and Maryland, and by a large body of volunteers from Virginia and Carolina, he advanced to Guilford Court-house, and offered battle to Cornwallis. On the 15th of March, an engagement took place. It ended in the defeat of the provincials, who sustained a loss of four hundred men.

Unable to follow up his victory from a scarcity of provisions, Cornwallis withdrew to Wilmington, while Greene halted at Deep River. In the hope of drawing Cornwallis in pursuit of him, and thus relieving North Carolina from the domination of the enemy, Greene determined to push forward into South Carolina, and attack Rawdon, who, with nine hundred men, was stationed at Camden. When the news of this movement reached

Cornwallis, Greene was already too far on his way to be pursued with any prospect of advantage. Leaving Rawdon, therefore, to maintain himself as well as he could, Cornwallis turned his steps northward, and penetrating into Virginia, formed a junction at Petersburg, on the 20th of May, with the British force under Arnold.

Receiving soon after a reinforcement of four regiments from New York, he so far outnumbered the troops under La Fayette, that the latter was compelled to retire from Richmond toward the Rappahannock, for the purpose of meeting Wayne, who was advancing to join the southern army with a detachment of the Pennsylvania line, amounting to nearly a thousand men.

Cornwallis at once started in pursuit, but finding it impossible to prevent a junction of the provincial forces, he turned his attention toward breaking up the detached posts in the interior of the state. A light infantry party under Lieutenant-colonel Simcoe was sent against Steuben, who was stationed with six hundred men at the junction of the Rivanna and Fluvanna Rivers, in charge of the military stores collected at that point; while Tarleton, with a body of cavalry, was ordered to push on to Charlottesville, where the assembly was in session, to seize the burgesses, and to attempt the capture of Jefferson, who had succeeded Patrick Henry as governor of the state, and resided in that vicinity. The expedition under Simcoe succeeded in forcing Steuben to retreat, and in destroying the laboratory and armory which had been placed under his protection. That under Tarleton was a partial failure. Seven of the burgesses, and twelve wagons, loaded with military stores fell into his hands, but Jefferson and the remainder of the delegates made good their escape. The two detachments having formed a junction, proceeded down the James River, ravaging the country on both sides of the stream, until they were called in to unite with the main army.

In the mean time, Clinton fearing an attack upon New York, by the combined American and French forces, had sent orders to Cornwallis to march toward the coast and take up such a position as would enable him to embark his troops in the event of their services being required. In obedience to these instructions, Cornwallis marced toward Williamsburg, which he entered on the 28th of June. La Fayette, reinforced by the levies under Steuben, hovered closely in his rear. At the crossing of the river opposite Jamestown, the provincial troops attacked the British with great spirit, but after a sharp action were beaten off with loss. On reaching Portsmouth, Cornwallis was met by fresh instructions from Sir Henry Clinton, directing him to take up a strong position and hold himself in readiness for future orders. Finding Portsmouth unsuited for such a purpose, he selected the peninsulas of York and Gloucester, as being more central and easier of access by the frigates and vessels which accompanied him. On the 1st of August, 1781, he concentrated the whole of his army at those points, which he strengthened soon after by a line of redoubts.

The grand drama of the revolution was now approaching its close. The expected arrival in the Chesapeake of a French fleet from the West Indies, enabled Washington to concert, with the Count de Rochambeau, a plan of operations, having for its object the capture of Cornwallis. Orders were immediately despatched to La Fayette, advising him of the intended movement, and directing him to occupy such a position as would prevent the retreat of the British into North Carolina.

After executing various manœuvres, by which the attention of Sir Henry Clinton was diverted from the real object of attack, the combined French and American forces marched, with great secrecy and rapidity, across the Jerseys to Philadelphia. Proceeding from the latter city to the head of Elk, in Maryland, they embarked in transports already collected at that point, and floating down the Chesapeake, formed a junction with the troops under La Fayette, at Williamsburg, toward the close of September.

In the mean time, the Count de Grasse had

succeeded in entering the Chesapeake with a fleet of twenty-six ships of the line, and several frigates. This large naval force was increased soon after by the arrival of the French squadron from Newport, under the Count de Barras.

The plan of operations having been definitely settled between Washington and the French commanders, the allied army, amounting to sixteen thousand men, marched from the camp at Williamsburg, and on the 30th of September, completely invested Yorktown, where the main body of the British force, eight thousand strong, had been concentrated.

During the first week in October, the besiegers were occupied in opening intrenchments, constructing breastworks, and in bringing up the heavy cannon and mortars from the ships. By the 8th of October, the first parallel, nearly two miles in extent, was completed. The next day, three batteries being prepared to open upon the town, Washington applied the match to the first gun with his own hands, and a furious cannonade immediately commenced. From the 10th to the 14th, the batteries of the allied forces kept up a tremendous and incessant firing upon the enemy, which was but feebly and ineffectually returned.

An event of unusual interest occurred on the 14th, in the simultaneous storming of two of the enemy's advanced redoubts, by two parties of picked men, the one body being wholly composed of French grenadiers and chasseurs, and the other of American light infantry. The van of the latter was commanded by Colonel Alexander Hamilton, who, after addressing his men in a speech of remarkable power and eloquence, led them to the attack with unloaded muskets, and carried the works at the point of the bayonet. The French storming party were equally successful. The captured redoubts being enclosed in the second parallel, the defences of the enemy gradually became untenable beneath the constant fire of the besiegers. On the night of the 16th, Cornwallis came to the desperate resolution of crossing his troops over to Gloucester Point, and by cutting his way through the small French force stationed there, endeavour to make good his retreat to New York. A part of his troops were actually embarked, but a violent storm arising, the boats, after being driven for some distance down the river, were compelled to put back to Yorktown.

Hemmed in on the one side by the French squadron, and on the other by the American and French land forces, with his defences nearly battered down, his ammunition almost exhausted, his provisions gone, and with no hope of receiving succour from Sir Henry Clinton, Cornwallis, on the 17th of October, proposed a cessation of hostilities, and the appointment of commissioners to arrange the terms of a capitulation. Articles were finally agreed upon, by which seven thousand British troops, with all the materiel of war, were surrendered to the American force; while the British ships, seamen, and naval stores, were given up to the combined French squadrons.

The final act of capitulation was peculiarly impressive. At the hour of noon, on the 19th of October, the combined army was drawn up facing each other, in two parallel lines, extending more than a mile in length. The Americans occupied the right side of the road, and the French the left. On horseback, at the head of the former, sat Washington, attended by his aids. At the head of the latter, was posted the Count Rochambeau and his suite. The French troops were in complete uniform. The American forces were variously habited, and bore evidence of the toils and privations through which they had struggled to a crowning triumph. Outside these lines, and thronging the fields beyond, was a prodigious concourse of spectators, attracted thither by the imposing nature of the ceremony about to be performed. About two o'clock, and in the midst of profound silence, the captive troops, newly uniformed, marched from the town, and defiled slowly between the lines formed for their reception, with shouldered arms, colours cased, and drums beating. All eyes were anxiously turned to gaze upon their leader, but under the plea of illness, Cornwallis had transferred the command to General O'Hara. When the latter arrived at the head of the line, he approached Washington and apologized for the absence of the commander-in-chief. General Lincoln was then directed to superintend the surrender, which was accomplished in a spacious field near by. The mortification of the British troops at being compelled to ground their arms in the presence of their conquerors, was so rudely manifested in the violence with which they divested themselves of their accoutrements, and threw down their muskets upon the pile, as to call forth a strong rebuke from Lincoln. Many of their officers were even more deeply affected. Colonel Abercrombie—the same who afterward distinguished himself in Egypt, and fell mortally wounded at the moment of victory—no sooner witnessed the surrender of his troops, then he withdrew rapidly, covering his face, and biting his sword.

But if the capitulation at Yorktown was a source of profound humiliation to the enemy, it was productive of the happiest results to the American colonies. The War of Independence was virtually closed. Hostilities continued however to be prosecuted in a languid manner, for some time after, in the south; but it soon became evident that England, growing weary of a contest from which she derived no hope of regaining her lost authority, was desirous of bringing it to a close. Accordingly, early in 1782, negotiations were opened for a peace, and on the 3d of February, 1783, a provisional treaty was concluded.

CHAPTER XXVI.

Close of the war—Exhausted condition of the country—Cession of the public lands—Convention at Philadelphia—Adoption of the Federal Constitution—Opposition in Virginia—Origin of the Federalists and Republicans—Fears respecting the constitution—Repudiation of British claims—Opinion of Washington—Increasing prosperity of the Union—Difficulties with France—Alien and sedition laws—Madison's resolutions—Slavery—Fears of Virginia—Acts passed in relation to—Difficulties with England—English and French decrees—Commercial distress—Declaration of war—Patriotism of Virginia—Peace proclaimed—Revisions of the Constitution—Servile insurrection—War with Mexico—Past condition of Virginia—Present prospects—System of internal improvement—Relation of Virginia to the states.

THE exhausted condition in which the several confederate states were left at the close of the war, rendered the first few years that followed a period of intense anxiety at home, and of curious speculation abroad. Burdened with debt, imperfectly united to each other, the commercial interests of the north conflicting with the agricultural interests of the south, at issue with respect to boundaries, and with the smaller states suspicious of the larger, the independence which had been achieved threatened to degenerate speedily into anarchy, unless the danger should be averted by mutual acts of concession and compromise. Happily, that patriotism which had stimulated them to stand shoulder to shoulder in the great struggle for independence, now animated them to rise superior to all sectional considerations, and to work together for the general good.

The first, and most striking evidence of harmonious action between the states, was the cession to the federal government of the western lands. In this surrender of territory, both from the magnitude of her claims, and the validity of her title, either by patent or by conquest, Virginia was peculiarly conspicuous. But, although one of the objects of this grant of lands to the federal government was for the purpose of providing means by their sale for the gradual liquidation of the national debt, the process was necessarily slow; and in the mean time, the people of the several states were reduced by the expenses of the war, by the depressed condition of trade, and by the claims of their British creditors, to a state of bankruptcy and partial insurrection.

The powers vested in the old continental congress being wholly insufficient to remedy evils of such magnitude, Virginia took the lead in proposing a re-organization of the federal government. Delegates from six states accordingly met at Annapolis, in September, 1786; but finding themselves too few in number to carry out effectively the wishes of their constituents, they resolved to adjourn, having first recommended a convention, to be composed of delegates from all the states, to meet at Philadelphia, the following May. This recommendation was finally carried into effect. On the 14th of May, 1787, the convention assembled at Philadelphia, elected Washington its presiding officer, and, after a stormy session of four months, adopted, on the 17th of September, the present Constitution of the United States.

The new constitution was immediately laid before the Continental Congress, then in session at New York, which, after some hesitation, transmitted a copy of it to each legislature, and recommended that state conventions should be called to decide upon its approval or rejection.

In the Virginia convention, which met at Richmond, in June, 1788, the ratification of the new constitution was strongly opposed by Patrick Henry and George Mason; but met with able advocates in Madison, Wythe, and Edmund Randolph. After a long and animated series of debates, all opposition was silenced, and on the 27th of June, the constitution was adopted by Virginia, subject, however, to certain amendments, which were to be submitted to the other states for approval.

But, although the constitution was finally ratified by the whole of the states, its friends were scarcely more numerous than its opponents. For a long time after it went into operation, a general doubt of its successful working pervaded the public mind. Some believed that it would lead to a breaking up of the confederation; some thought the powers intrusted to congress and the executive were too extensive; while others contended that the executive authority was altogether too weak and dependent. These opposite opinions resulted in the formation of two great parties, the friends of the constitution acquiring the name of Federalists, while those who were hostile to many of its provisions, assumed the title of Republicans.

The Virginia assembly, which met in November, 1788, were so fully impressed with the belief that the constitution required amendment in many of its most essential articles, that, following the example of New York, they framed an address to the federal Congress, advocating the call of a new convention, for the purpose of revising that instrument. Fortunately, perhaps, for the integrity of the Union, the suggestion was not adopted. The moderate men of both parties, conscious of the difficulty which had attended the framing of the system of government just established, were unwilling to retrace their steps over ground so dangerous. Some changes they conceded to be necessary, and accordingly, at the session of the first Congress in 1789, out of seventeen amendments proposed, twelve passed both houses, ten of which, being subsequently sanctioned by a majority of the state legislatures, became a part of the Constitution.

Notwithstanding these well-meant efforts at conciliation, several of the states were far from being satisfied. Prominent among these stood Virginia. Fearful that the creation of a strong central power would tend to weaken the sovereignty of the states, many of the most eminent men, at the head of whom was Patrick Henry, adopted, from the first, opinions strongly anti-federal. The great mass of the people of the state also arrayed themselves on the same side, being insensibly led into opposition by the dread of having to pay the old debts due to British merchants, for the collection of which the federal constitution was supposed to furnish additional facilities. These debts, amounting in the aggregate to ten millions of dollars, "had become hereditary from father to son for many generations, so that the planters were a species of property annexed to certain mercantile houses in London." Beggared as they already were from losses sustained during the war, and from the expenses of a contest so protracted, many of the planters, acting under the impulse of self-preservation, were not unwilling to repudiate claims, which they felt themselves incapable of liquidating without reducing their families to absolute penury.

The prevalence of a similar feeling, induced many of the state legislatures to pass laws to prevent the collection of debts by British merchants; and as these acts were in direct violation of the fourth article of the treaty, Great Britain refused to surrender the western and north-western posts until the claims of her subjects were satisfactorily adjusted.

The fine moral sense of Washington could not witness this infraction of the treaty without openly protesting against it. He deeply regretted that Great Britain should have any pretext for still retaining possession of any part of the territory confessedly belonging to the United States, and of exercising thereby a dangerous control over the Indian tribes which were scattered along the frontiers. "The distresses of individuals," said he, "are to be alleviated by industry and frugality, and not by a relaxation of the laws, or by a sacrifice of the rights of others."

Notwithstanding the ominous misgivings of many true patriots, the country slowly recovered from the extreme prostration into which it had fallen, and the prediction of Washington, that the day was coming when America, weak as she then was, would have some weight in the scale of empire, was in the sure process of fulfilment.

The eight years during which that great and good man occupied the presidential chair, were years of trouble and difficulty; but it was upon the succeeding administration of the elder Adams that the storm of political opposition most fiercely vented itself.

From the period of the arrival of Genet, as ambassador of the new French republic, in 1793, to the year 1798, the American nation had been subjected by that ill regulated power to a series of insults and injuries. Repeated efforts at redress having signally failed, a war appeared at length to be inevitable. For the purpose of protecting the administration at this crisis from internal and external enemies, the famous, but unwise, alien and sedition laws were passed.

By the first act, in relation to aliens, no foreigner could become a citizen unless he had previously resided in the United States for a period of fourteen years.

By a second act, limited in its operation to two years, the president was authorized to order out of the country all such aliens as he might judge dangerous to the peace and safety of the United States; while by a third, all aliens, resident in the country after war had been declared, upon a proclamation issued by the president, might be apprehended, or secured, or removed.

The sedition law, which was to continue in force for three years, was not less stringent. The first section imposed a fine not exceeding five thousand dollars, imprisonment from six months to five years, and binding to good behaviour at the discretion of the court, "for any persons unlawfully to combine and conspire together, with intent to oppose any measures of the government of the United States, directed by proper authority, or to impede the operation of any law of the United States, or to intimidate, or prevent any person holding office from the execution of his trust, or to commit, advise, or attempt to procure any insurrection, riot, unlawful assembly, or combination."

These laws met with the most vehement opposition in Virginia. A number of resolutions, drawn up by Jefferson, had already passed the legislature of Kentucky, in which the doctrine of state rights was advocated with great boldness and ability, and the alien and sedition laws declared void and of no force. In December, 1798, resolutions of a similar character, drafted by Madison, were adopted by the legislature of Virginia.

The preamble to these resolutions declared that the powers of the federal government resulted only from a compact to which the states were parties; and that in case of the exercise of powers not granted by the compact, the states possessed the right to interpose for the correction of the evil.

After expressing "deep regret at a spirit manifested by the federal government to enlarge its powers by a forced construction of the constitutional charter, and by an improper interpretation of certain phrases, to consolidate the states into one sovereignty, the obvious tendency and result of which would be, to transform the present republican system into an absolute or at best a mixed monarchy," the resolutions closed with a strong protest against the alien and sedition laws, as "palpable and alarming infractions of the constitution."

But these opinions found only a partial support in the other states of the Union; and subsequent experience has shown that the fears, which were at that day so earnestly entertained by many of the best and purest statesmen of the republic, were based upon an incorrect appreciation of the intelligence and capacity of the people.

From this period, until the war of 1812, the history of the State of Virginia presents but few points of interest to the general reader. Silently increasing in wealth and numbers, the great mass of the population gradually became warmly attached to that system of federal government which at first they had regarded with so many ominous misgivings. The only source of remaining doubt arose from sectional differences in regard to slavery. The abolition, therefore, of the slave trade by Congress, was not viewed by any of the southern states without serious alarm, lest it should be followed by measures more directly interfering with that species of property. This feeling of insecurity was increased in Virginia by the consciousness that two attempts at servile insurrection had already occurred during the years 1799 and 1801. It influenced the legislature of 1805 to pass a law, which authorized the apprehension and sale of all emancipated slaves remaining in the state for twelve months after obtaining their freedom; forbade the education of orphan coloured children left in charge of the overseers of the poor; and ordered such free blacks as entered the state, to be sent back to the places from whence they came.

A deeper source of anxiety arose soon after in the critical relations of the United States with regard to foreign powers, but more especially with England.

After a long and sanguinary war, the genius of Napoleon had subjected every nation to his arbitrary will, with the exception of Great Britain. The fierce struggle for supremacy between these two powers led to infractions of the rights of neutrals, which were endured for a long time by the Americans, for the sake of the profitable carrying trade which the war in Europe had thrown into their hands.

At length England, jealous of the growing naval power of the United States, determined to check its increase by laying many of the French ports under embargo, and by declaring the vessels of neutrals bearing French products to be lawful prize. Napoleon retaliated by the famous

Berlin decree, which was issued from the battle-field of Jena on the 21st of November, 1806. This decree declared the British Islands in a state of blockade, and prohibited all trade in English merchandise.

The effect of these acts was to put almost an entire stop to commercial enterprise in the United States; but the hope was still entertained that, either by negotiation or remonstrance, the causes for complaint would be eventually removed. Such hopes proved fallacious. Difficulties arose soon after with England in relation to the right of impressment, which an unprovoked attack upon the Chesapeake by the English frigate Leopard, off the Capes of Virginia, complicated still further.

The commercial states were not, however, as yet prepared to consent to a declaration of war, and various ineffectual measures were resorted to, during the four succeeding years, in the effort to avoid an appeal to arms.

In 1807, the ports of the United States were closed against British vessels; but the great commercial distress which the restriction occasioned, led to its suspension at the ensuing session of congress. In 1809, a more comprehensive act was passed by congress, which prohibited all intercourse with Great Britain, France, or their dependencies.

These acts proving ineffectual, and all attempts

at an amicable adjustment of the points at issue having been met by evasions or delays, the patience of the people became exhausted, and on the 18th of June, 1812, congress formally declared war.

In this declaration, as in the measures by which it was preceded, Virginia yielded a cordial support to the national executive; and upon the commencement of hostilities, her patriotism continued to display itself in the alacrity with which volunteers from all parts of the state enrolled themselves for the defence of the country. For a long time the war was confined principally to the frontiers and the ocean; but when at length, in the summer of 1814, the enemy entered the Chesapeake, and attempted to ravage the borders of Virginia by various petty predatory incursions, the resistance offered by the local militia was worthy of the ancient reputation of the state.

Hostilities terminated a few months later. On the 24th of December, 1814, a treaty of peace was signed at Ghent, which was ratified by the United States on the 17th of February, 1815.

The subsequent history of Virginia is not marked by any event of historical importance until the year 1829, when a general convention was called for the purpose of revising the old state constitution. The number of eminent men who occupied seats in this convention, gave a peculiar interest and importance to the minutes of its proceedings; for, prominent among its members were ex-presidents Monroe and Madison, and Chief Justice Marshall—all three of whom had taken part in the formation of the original constitution.

It might have been supposed that the labours of a convention, composed almost wholly of the most distinguished men in Virginia, would have resulted in framing a constitution so well adapted to the wants of the people as to need no subsequent revision for a long series of years. Unfortunately, the excess of intellectual force appears to have been fatal to the production of an instrument so desirable. Although it was ratified by the people, its many imperfections rendered it so constant a source of dissatisfaction, that a third convention was called in 1850, which, after a warm and protracted session, effected a thorough revision of the previous constitution, and allayed, to a considerable degree, the dissatisfaction of the people of Western Virginia by the adoption of a different and more equitable basis of representation.

During the year 1831, a great excitement was created throughout the state by a servile insurrection in the county of Southampton, which, originating in the fanaticism of one Nat Turner, led to the massacre of thirty-five persons; but the terror created by this sudden and sanguinary outbreak, was speedily allayed by the arrest and punishment of the principal offenders.

In the Mexican war, which broke out in 1845, large numbers of volunteers from Virginia joined the armies of the Republic, and assisted in gaining that wonderful succession of victories which, from the banks of the Rio del Norte to the pass of Angostura, and from the ancient city of Vera Cruz to the walls of Mexico, were untarnished by a single defeat.

Almost wholly engaged in agricultural pursuits, the people of Virginia have not, until within the last few years, become sufficiently aware of the necessity of adopting that important system of internal improvements, for which many of her less wealthy, but more energetic sister states, have rendered themselves so distinguished. The public mind, however, has at length become fully aroused from a condition of apathetic indifference, to one of active inquiry. Works of great magnitude, based upon the excellent credit of the state, are already projected; while the noble water-power of the James River, for many years so unwisely neglected, is beginning to attract that attention from practical business men, which its admirable capacity for manufacturing purposes has so long deserved.

The earliest settled of all the confederated states, Virginia, justly regarded as the birth-place of a great nation, has become endeared to the rest of the Union by the romantic incidents connected with her early career; and above all, by the steadfast manner in which she has always defended her rights and privileges, as displayed in Bacon's rebellion, in her systematic endeavours to retrench the assumed prerogatives of her royal governors, and in the fearless ardour with which she placed herself, first among the foremost, in constant and unwavering opposition to British oppression.

THE END.

STEREOTYPED BY L. JOHNSON AND CO.
PHILADELPHIA.

BALDWIN'S PRONOUNCING GAZETTEER.

A PRONOUNCING GAZETTEER:

Containing Topographical, Statistical, and other Information, of the more important Places in the known World, from the most recent and authentic Sources.

BY THOMAS BALDWIN,

Assisted by several other Gentlemen.

To which is added an APPENDIX, containing more than TEN THOUSAND ADDITIONAL NAMES, chiefly of the small Towns and Villages, &c., of the United States and of Mexico.

NINTH EDITION, WITH A SUPPLEMENT,

Giving the Pronunciation of near two thousand names, besides those pronounced in the Original Work: Forming in itself a Complete Vocabulary of Geographical Pronunciation.

ONE VOLUME 12MO.—PRICE, $1 50.

FIELD'S SCRAP BOOK.—NEW EDITION.

Literary and Miscellaneous Scrap Book.

Consisting of Tales and Anecdotes—Biographical, Historical, Moral, Religious, and Sentimental Pieces, in Prose and Poetry.

COMPILED BY WM. FIELDS.

SECOND EDITION, REVISED AND IMPROVED.

In one handsome 8vo. Volume. Price, $2 00.

AUNT PHILLIS'S CABIN;

OR, SOUTHERN LIFE AS IT IS.

BY MRS. MARY H. EASTMAN.

PRICE, 50 AND 75 CENTS.

This volume presents a picture of Southern Life, taken at different points of view from the one occupied by the authoress of "*Uncle Tom's Cabin.*" The writer, being a native of the South, is familiar with the many varied aspects assumed by domestic servitude in that sunny region, and therefore feels competent to give pictures of "Southern Life, as it is."

Pledged to no clique or party, and free from the pressure of any and all extraneous influences, she has written her book with a view to its truthfulness; and the public at the North, as well as at the South, will find in "Aunt Phillis's Cabin" not the distorted picture of an interested painter, but the faithful transcript of a Daguerreotypist.

THE CONFESSIONS OF A HOUSEKEEPER.

BY MRS. JOHN SMITH.

WITH THIRTEEN HUMOROUS ILLUSTRATIONS.

One Volume 12mo. Price 50 Cents.

THE HUMAN BODY AND ITS CONNEXION WITH MAN.

ILLUSTRATED BY THE PRINCIPAL ORGANS.

BY JAMES JOHN GARTH WILKINSON.

Member of the Royal College of Surgeons of England.

IN ONE VOLUME 12MO.—PRICE, $1 25.

WHEELER'S HISTORY OF NORTH CAROLINA.

Historical Sketches

OF NORTH CAROLINA,

From 1584 to 1851.

Compiled from Original Records, Official Documents, and Traditional Statements; with Biographical Sketches of her Distinguished Statesmen, Jurists, Lawyers, Soldiers, Divines, &c.

BY JOHN H. WHEELER,

Late Treasurer of the State.

IN ONE VOLUME OCTAVO.—PRICE, $2 00.

THE NORTH CAROLINA READER:

CONTAINING A HISTORY AND DESCRIPTION OF NORTH CAROLINA, SELECTIONS IN PROSE AND VERSE, (MANY OF THEM BY EMINENT CITIZENS OF THE STATE), HISTORICAL AND CHRONOLOGICAL TABLES,

And a Variety of Miscellaneous Information and Statistics.

BY C. H. WILEY.

"My own green land for ever!
Land of the beautiful and brave—
The freeman's home—the martyr's grave."

Illustrated with Engravings, and designed for Families and Schools.

One Volume 12mo. Price $1.00.

Splendid Illustrated Books, suitable for Gifts for the Holidays.

The Iris: An Original Souvenir for any Year.

EDITED BY PROF. JOHN S. HART.

WITH TWELVE SPLENDID ILLUMINATIONS, ALL FROM ORIGINAL DESIGNS.

THE DEW-DROP: A TRIBUTE OF AFFECTION.

WITH NINE STEEL ENGRAVINGS.

GEMS FROM THE SACRED MINE.

WITH TEN STEEL PLATES AND ILLUMINATIONS.

THE POET'S OFFERING.

WITH FOURTEEN STEEL PLATES AND ILLUMINATIONS.

THE STANDARD EDITIONS OF THE POETS.

WITH ILLUSTRATIONS.

LORD AND LADY HARCOURT:
OR, COUNTRY HOSPITALITIES.

BY CATHARINE SINCLAIR,

Author of "Jane Bouverie," "The Business of Life," "Modern Accomplishments," &c., &c.

One Volume 12mo. Price 50 cents, paper; cloth, fine, 75 cents.

William's New Map of the United States,

ON ROLLERS.

SIZE TWO AND A HALF BY THREE FEET.

A new map of the United States, upon which are delineated its vast works of Internal Communication, Routes across the Continent, &c., showing also Canada and the Island of Cuba,

BY W. WILLIAMS.

This Map is handsomely colored and mounted on rollers, and will be found a beautiful and useful ornament to the Counting-House and Parlor, as well as the School-Room. Price Two Dollars.

SCHOOLCRAFTS GREAT NATIONAL WORK

ON THE

Indian Tribes of the United States.

PART SECOND—QUARTO.

WITH EIGHTY BEAUTIFUL ILLUSTRATIONS ON STEEL,

Engraved in the first style of the art, from Drawings by Capt. Eastman, U.S.A.

PRICE, FIFTEEN DOLLARS.

COCKBURN'S LIFE OF LORD JEFFREY.

LIFE OF LORD JEFFREY,

WITH

A SELECTION FROM HIS CORRESPONDENCE,

BY LORD COCKBURN,

One of the Judges of the Court of Sessions in Scotland.

2 vols. 12mo. Price, $2 50.

ROMANCE OF NATURAL HISTORY;

OR, WILD SCENES AND WILD HUNTERS.

WITH NUMEROUS ILLUSTRATIONS, ONE VOLUME OCTAVO, CLOTH.

BY C. W. WEBBER,

Author of "Old Hicks the Guide," "Shot in the Eye," &c.

PRICE, TWO DOLLARS.

THE LIFE OF WILLIAM PENN,

WITH

SELECTIONS FROM HIS CORRESPONDENCE AND AUTOBIOGRAPHY

BY SAMUEL M. JANNEY.

Second Edition, Revised. Price, Two Dollars.

LIPPINCOTT'S

CABINET HISTORIES OF THE STATES,

CONSISTING OF A SERIES OF

Cabinet Histories of all the States of the Union,

TO EMBRACE A VOLUME FOR EACH STATE.

We have so far completed all our arrangements, as to be able to issue the whole series in the shortest possible time consistent with its careful literary production. SEVERAL VOLUMES ARE NOW READY FOR SALE. The talented authors who have engaged to write these Histories, are no strangers in the literary world.

"These most tastefully printed and bound volumes form the first instalment of a series of State Histories, which, without superseding the bulkier and more expensive works of the same character, may enter household channels from which the others would be excluded by their cost and magnitude."

"In conciseness, clearness, skill of arrangement, and graphic interest, they are a most excellent earnest of those to come. They are eminently adapted both to interest and instruct, and should have a place in the family library of every American."—*N. Y. Courier and Enquirer.*

New Themes for the Protestant Clergy;

CREEDS WITHOUT CHARITY, THEOLOGY WITHOUT HUMANITY, AND PROTESTANTISM WITHOUT CHRISTIANITY;

With Notes by the Editor on the Literature of Charity, Population, Pauperism, Political Economy, and Protestantism.

PRICE, ONE DOLLAR.

SIMPSON'S MILITARY JOURNAL.

JOURNAL OF A MILITARY RECONNOISSANCE FROM SANTA FE NEW MEXICO, TO THE NAVAJO COUNTRY,

BY JAMES H. SIMPSON, A. M.,

FIRST LIEUTENANT CORPS OF TOPOGRAPHICAL ENGINEERS.

WITH 75 COLOURED ILLUSTRATIONS.

One volume, octavo. Price, Three Dollars.

In Press,

A NEW AND COMPLETE

GAZETTEER OF THE UNITED STATES.

It will furnish the fullest and most recent information respecting the Geography Statistics, and present state of improvement, of every part of this great Republic, particularly of

TEXAS, CALIFORNIA, OREGON, NEW MEXICO,

&c. The work will be issued as soon as the complete official returns of the present Census are received.

THE ABOVE WORK WILL BE FOLLOWED BY

A UNIVERSAL GAZETTEER,

OR GEOGRAPHICAL DICTIONARY,

of the most complete and comprehensive character. It will be compiled from the best English, French, and German authorities, and will be published the moment that the returns of the present census of Europe can be obtained.

History of the Mormons

OF UTAH,

THEIR DOMESTIC POLITY AND THEOLOGY,

BY J. W. GUNNISON,

U. S. CORPS TOPOGRAPHICAL ENGINEERS.

WITH ILLUSTRATIONS, IN ONE VOLUME DEMI-OCTAVO.

REPORT OF A GEOLOGICAL SURVEY OF WISCONSIN, IOWA, AND MINNESOTA,

AND INCIDENTALLY OF A PORTION OF NEBRASKA TERRITORY,

MADE UNDER INSTRUCTIONS FROM THE U. S. TREASURY DEPARTM'T

BY DAVID DALE OWEN,

United States' Geologist.

WITH OVER 150 ILLUSTRATIONS ON STEEL AND WOOD.

TWO VOLUMES, QUARTO. PRICE $10 00.

MERCHANTS' MEMORANDUM BOOK,

WITH LISTS OF ALL GOODS PURCHASED BY COUNTRY MERCHANTS, &c.

One volume, 18mo., Leather cover. Price, 50 cents.

THE ABBOTSFORD EDITION

OF

The Waverley Novels,

Printed upon fine white Paper, with new and beautiful Type,

FROM THE LAST ENGLISH EDITION,

EMBRACING

THE AUTHOR'S LATEST CORRECTIONS, NOTES, ETC.,

Complete in 12 volumes, demi-octavo, neatly bound in cloth,

With Illustrations,

FOR ONLY TWELVE DOLLARS,

CONTAINING

WAVERLEY, or 'Tis Sixty Years Since...THE FORTUNES OF NIGEL.
GUY MANNERING...PEVERIL OF THE PEAK.
THE ANTIQUARY...QUENTIN DURWARD.
THE BLACK DWARF...ST. RONAN'S WELL.
OLD MORTALITY...REDGAUNTLET.
ROB ROY...THE BETROTHED.
THE HEART OF MID-LOTHIAN...THE TALISMAN.
THE BRIDE OF LAMMERMOOR...WOODSTOCK.
A LEGEND OF MONTROSE...THE HIGHLAND WIDOW, &c.
IVANHOE...THE FAIR MAID OF PERTH.
THE MONASTERY...ANNE OF GEIERSTEIN.
THE ABBOT...COUNT ROBERT OF PARIS.
KENILWORTH...CASTLE DANGEROUS.
THE PIRATE...SURGEON'S DAUGHTER, &c.

Any of the above Novels sold, in Paper Covers, at Fifty Cents each.

ALSO,

THE SAME EDITION

OF

THE WAVERLEY NOVELS,

In Twelve Volumes, Royal Octavo, on Superfine Paper, with

THREE HUNDRED CHARACTERISTIC AND BEAUTIFUL ILLUSTRATIONS.

ELEGANTLY BOUND IN CLOTH, GILT.

Price, Only Twenty-Four Dollars.

FROST'S JUVENILE SERIES.

TWELVE VOLUMES, 16mo., WITH FIVE HUNDRED ENGRAVINGS.

WALTER O'NEILL, OR THE PLEASURE OF DOING GOOD. 25 Engravings.
JUNKER SCHOTT, and other Stories. 6 Engravings.
THE LADY OF THE LURLEI, and other Stories. 12 Engravings.
ELLEN'S BIRTHDAY, and other Stories. 20 Engravings.
HERMAN, and other Stories. 9 Engravings.
KING TREGEWALL'S DAUGHTER, and other Stories. 16 Engr's.
THE DROWNED BOY, and other Stories. 6 Engravings.
THE PICTORIAL RHYME-BOOK. 122 Engravings.
THE PICTORIAL NURSERY BOOK. 117 Engravings.
THE GOOD CHILD'S REWARD. 115 Engravings.
ALPHABET OF QUADRUPEDS. 26 Engravings.
ALPHABET OF BIRDS. 26 Engravings.

PRICE, TWENTY-FIVE CENTS EACH.

The above popular and attractive series of New Juveniles for the Young, are sold together or separately.

THE MILLINER AND THE MILLIONAIRE.

BY MRS. REBECCA HICKS,

(Of Virginia,) Author of "The Lady Killer," &c. 1 vol. 12mo. Price, 37 1-2 cents.

STANSBURY'S
EXPEDITION TO THE GREAT SALT LAKE.

AN EXPLORATION
OF THE VALLEY OF THE GREAT SALT LAKE
OF UTAH,

CONTAINING ITS GEOGRAPHY, NATURAL HISTORY, MINERALOGICAL RESOURCES, ANALYSIS OF ITS WATERS, AND AN AUTHENTIC ACCOUNT OF

THE MORMON SETTLEMENT.

Also, A Reconnoissance of a New Route through the Rocky Mountains, with Seventy Beautiful Illustrations, from Drawings taken on the spot, and two large and accurate Maps of that region.

BY HOWARD STANSBURY,

Captain Topographical Engineers. 2 vols. royal octavo. Price $5 00.

The Hunter Naturalist, A Romance of Sporting;

OR, WILD SCENES AND WILD HUNTERS,

BY C. W. WEBBER,

Author of "Shot in the Eye," "Old Hicks the Guide," "Gold Mines of the Gila," &c.

ONE VOLUME, ROYAL OCTAVO.

ILLUSTRATED WITH FORTY BEAUTIFUL ENGRAVINGS, RROM ORIGINAL DRAWINGS, MANY OF WHICH ARE COLOURED.

PRICE FIVE DOLLARS.

A REVIEW

OF

"NEW THEMES FOR THE PROTESTANT CLERGY."

ONE VOLUME 12mo.

Price, paper, 25 cents. Cloth, 50 cents.

THE BIBLE IN THE COUNTING-HOUSE.

BY H. A. BOARDMAN, D.D.,

AUTHOR OF "THE BIBLE IN THE FAMILY."

One vol. 12mo., cloth. Price One Dollar.

AUTOBIOGRAPHY OF A NEW CHURCHMAN.

BY JOHN A. LITTLE.

ONE VOLUME 12mo. PRICE 75 CENTS.

MILTON'S WORKS—NEW AND COMPLETE EDITION.

Milton's Poetical Works,

WITH A LIFE, DISSERTATION, INDEX, AND NOTES,

BY PROF. C. D. CLEVELAND.

ONE VOLUME ROYAL 12mo., CLOTH. PRICE $1 25.

UNIFORM AND DRESS

OF THE

ARMY OF THE UNITED STATES.

WITH COLOURED ILLUSTRATIONS.

QUARTO, CLOTH. PRICE FIVE DOLLARS.

UNIFORM AND DRESS

OF THE

NAVY OF THE UNITED STATES.

WITH COLOURED ILLUSTRATIONS.

QUARTO, CLOTH. PRICE FIVE DOLLARS.

THE FISCAL HISTORY OF TEXAS:

EMBRACING AN ACCOUNT OF ITS REVENUES, DEBTS, AND CURRENCY, FROM THE COMMENCEMENT OF THE REVOLUTION IN 1834, TO 1851-2,

WITH REMARKS ON AMERICAN DEBTS.

BY WM. M. GOUGE,

Author of "A Short History of Paper Money and Banking in the United States."

In one vol. 8vo., cloth. Price $1 50.

INGERSOLL'S HISTORY of the SECOND WAR:

A HISTORY OF THE SECOND WAR BETWEEN THE UNITED STATES AND GREAT BRITAIN.

BY CHARLES J. INGERSOLL.

Second series. 2 volumes, 8vo. Price $4 00.

These two volumes, which embrace the hostile transactions between the United States and Great Britain during the years 1814 and '15, complete Mr. Ingersoll's able work on the Second or "Late War," as it has usually been called. A great deal of new and valuable matter has been collected by the author from original sources, and is now first introduced to the public.

A PRACTICAL TREATISE ON BUSINESS;

OR, HOW TO GET, SAVE, SPEND, GIVE, LEND, AND BEQUEATH MONEY

WITH AN INQUIRY INTO THE CHANCES OF SUCCESS AND CAUSES OF FAILURE IN BUSINESS.

BY EDWIN T. FREEDLY.

Also, Prize Essays, Statistics, Miscellanies, and numerous private letters from successful and distinguished business men.

12mo., cloth. Price One Dollar.

The object of this treatise is fourfold. First, the elevation of the business character, and to define clearly the limits within which it is not only proper but obligatory to get money. Secondly, to lay down the principles which must be observed to insure success, and what must be avoided to escape failure. Thirdly, to give the mode of management in certain prominent pursuits adopted by the most successful, from which men in all kinds of business may derive profitable hints. Fourthly, to afford a work of solid interest to those who read without expectation of pecuniary benefit.

TRUTHS ILLUSTRATED by GREAT AUTHORS.

A DICTIONARY OF OVER FOUR THOUSAND AIDS TO REFLECTION —QUOTATIONS OF MAXIMS, METAPHORS, COUNSELS, CAUTIONS, APHORISMS, PROVERBS, &c. &c., IN PROSE AND VERSE;

COMPILED FROM SHAKSPEARE, AND OTHER GREAT WRITERS, FROM THE EARLIEST AGES TO THE PRESENT TIME.

A new edition, with American additions and revisions.

ONE VOLUME, CROWN OCTAVO, VARIOUS BINDINGS.

The Footpath and Highway;

OR,

WANDERINGS OF AN AMERICAN IN GT. BRITAIN,

IN 1851 AND '52.

BY BENJAMIN MORAN.

This volume embodies the observations of the author, made during eight months' wanderings, as a correspondent for American Journals; and as he travelled much on foot, differs essentially from those on the same countries, by other writers. The habits, manners, customs, and condition of the people have been carefully noted, and his views of them are given in clear, bold language. His remarks take a wide range, and as he visited every county in England but three, there will be much in the work of a novel and instructive character.

One vol. 12mo. Price $1 25.

www.ingramcontent.com/pod-product-compliance
Lightning Source LLC
LaVergne TN
LVHW010205110826
845151LV00002B/605
* 9 7 8 1 4 2 5 5 3 6 2 3 7 *